The Noughtie Girl's Guide to Feminism

The Noughtie Girl's Guide to Feminism

Ellie Levenson

ONEWORLD

OXFORD

A Oneworld Paperback Original
Published by Oneworld Publications 2009

ISBN 978–1–85168–683–4

Typeset by Jayvee, Trivandrum, India
Cover design by designedbydavid.co.uk
Printed and bound in Great Britain by the CPI Group

Oneworld Publications
185 Banbury Road
Oxford OX2 7AR
England
www.oneworld-publications.com

Learn more about Oneworld. Join our mailing list to
find out about our latest titles and special offers at:

www.oneworld-publications.com

Contents

Quiz – are you a noughtie girl?

1. A good looking, witty, handsome, single man offers to buy you a very expensive dinner. Do you …
    A. Giggle, accept and afterwards kiss him on the cheek and say goodbye. After twenty more such evenings he should present you with a diamond ring.
    B. Offer to pay half, and when he refuses throw your coffee over him and yell 'There's no need for misogyny you bastard' before storming out.
    C. Accept and take a spare pair of knickers and a toothbrush with you in case you decide to go back to his.

2. Your beloved boyfriend suggests that it would be a good time to have a chat about 'the future', and wonders whether you fancy looking at wedding venues this weekend. Do you …
    A. Give him your dad's phone number and say you think he should have a chat with him first.

    B. Say you don't believe in outdated patriarchal traditions and when he looks upset dump him for being a wimp.

    C. Take time out to think about whether this is a future you want, and then do whatever feels right for you.

3. Your five-year-old daughter wants to decorate her room all in pink. Do you …

    A. Say you don't really think pink is girly enough and suggest she add glitter and flower stencils to the wish-list and by the way, doesn't she think she's old enough to start wearing make-up now?

    B. Say you've never bought her a pink item in her life, why would you start doing so now, and make a note to send her to a feminist consciousness raising summer camp this year.

    C. Agree, with the condition that she repeats the mantra 'Pink is not only for girls and girls can like colours other than pink' ten times a day before school.

4. Your boss says you have great management potential and suggests you apply for promotion. Do you …

    A. Blush furiously and then refuse politely. How would you manage to get home in time to make dinner if you had all that extra work?

    B. Say that's kind but you don't want to move up the company, you want to run it, and that you'll be launching a women only takeover bid at the next AGM.

C. Have a think about it and decide whether this fits in with your general work–life balance before asking for an informal chat about the extra responsibilities and the extra money.

5. Your partner offers to take the male contraceptive pill as part of a trial study so you can give your body a break from the extra hormones. Do you …

   A. Say 'Actually honey, women's bodies are designed this way in order to bear children. We should be stopping contraception altogether and making a family – that's all I want in life.'

   B. Say 'Why make the empty gesture, every time I sleep with you the act of penetration feels like a crime against women anyway?'

   C. Say yes, but because you don't trust him to remember you secretly get fitted with a coil as well.

6. There is a building site at the end of the road and every time you walk past it you get wolf-whistled. Do you …

   A. Think to yourself 'What nice men', and return later that day with a tray of homemade lemonade for them.

   B. Flip them the finger and then call the council when you get home and ask that they be given an ASBO.

   C. Put your head down and ignore them while tutting to yourself – but secretly you feel flattered.

Results

Mostly A

Feminism probably isn't something you have given much thought to in the past. Perhaps you've felt alienated by the concept or you think all feminists have to cut their hair short. But you probably are a noughtie girl, because you believe that everybody should be able to make their own choices just as you have made yours. Read on to find out about some of the areas in which women make choices every day, and why yours are as valid as anyone else's.

Mostly B

You are definitely a noughtie girl – you are a feminist and proud of it. Not only that but you've read all the literature and probably set up a women's group of your very own to discuss the failings of men and society generally. But feminism has changed this millennium – noughtie girls know there's more than one way to be a feminist, and that wearing pink doesn't necessarily rule you out. Read on to find out how women in the noughties are changing the face of feminism.

Mostly C

You're a typical noughtie girl already – full of contradictions and determined not to succumb to anyone's view of feminism other than your own. Read on to see what similarities and differences you have with other noughtie girls, and to find out why your way is the future of feminism.

Acknowledgements

S pecial thanks to Ros Levenson, my mum, who gives me so many ideas that everything I write is effectively written jointly using my first name and her surname, unless it is wrong of course, in which case it is written solely by me, and to Richard Messingham, my husband, who I love dearly and who has shown patience and tolerance in bundles and who, luckily for me, has enough of these for both of us.

Also particular thanks to Jessica Asato for reading a draft and giving me lots of food for thought, Sarah Cousins for brilliant insights and helpful comments, Sue Lewis for her many interesting suggestions and Howard and Joe Levenson for helping to create a feminist friendly house to grow up in.

Many other people have helped me with this book by sharing anecdotes and ideas, in particular Alix O'Neill, Beth Breeze, Catherine Dean, Claire Kober, Diane Roxburgh, Emma Carr, Jane Clay, Jane Stobart, Jennifer Gerber, John Springford, Kate Groucutt, Kate Hilpern, Katharine Whitehorn, Laura Powell, Linda Jones, Louise Gale, Lucy Brett, Meabh Ritchie, Megan Pacey, Naomi Westland, Paul Richards, Rachel Miles, Rebecca

Rykalski, Victoria Neumark-Jones and Will Mcdonald. Thanks also to the Goldsmiths students who have helped me with this book and to all of the local Fabian Society branches who invited me to speak to them about this subject and discussed the issues with me. And of course thanks to anybody I have forgotten to name here and all of the people who have encouraged me and enquired about this book's progress. None of this means any of them agree with anything I have written. Thanks also to my editors at the *Guardian*, the *Independent*, the *Observer*, *New Statesman* and *Cosmopolitan* where some of the ideas and thoughts I have written in this book were first published.

And of course thank you to Jonathan Conway, my agent, who is encouraging, honest and always returns my calls (so far), and to Marsha Filion, Lizzie Curtin, Dawn Sackett, Kate Smith and the fantastic team at Oneworld.

Introduction

I gave a speech at my best friend's wedding recently. It was a long engagement so I had sixteen months to prepare. During this time I thought a lot about what I wanted to say. Amid the usual stories of how we met and some funny anecdotes about her life, I wanted to pay tribute to her character. Sarah is, I said:

> Thoughtful, always appropriate, great fun, inquisitive, adventurous and generous. Sarah is a feminist, a great conversationalist, a good cook, a brilliant keeper of secrets. She offers advice when it's needed and manages not to when it's not. She's interesting and interested and hardworking and dedicated. She is witty, tolerant and kind.

All of this came easily to me – she really is that great. Except for one word. Feminist. I didn't doubt that Sarah is a feminist, even though her dad had escorted her up the aisle and she had just vowed to dedicate her life to a man. After all, Sarah was using her wedding to make many feminist statements. She would not be changing her surname. She would be giving a speech and she had a best woman – me – just as her husband had a best man. She deliberately began her own speech by subverting the traditional 'My wife and I …' with 'My husband and I …'

But I still had doubts about offending an audience that I'd mainly never met. When I had written my speech I read it through. And I kept coming back to the word feminist. I thought about it for some time, then decided to say it anyway. Sarah was delighted.

Why is it that I was worried about using this word? I grew up believing that feminism was something to be proud of, not something to keep hidden. In fact it was Sarah who, unwittingly perhaps, helped me to articulate my thoughts about feminism. I was once trying to explain to her about my religion (I'm a non-practising Jew) and how it has an impact on my life. It is everything and nothing, I told her. I don't think very much about being Jewish on the one hand, but on the other I think about it all the time. It impacts on my humour, my family relationships, my interests, the food I like and the way I look. 'It sounds like being a woman' Sarah said. And she was right.

I don't think every second of the day about the fact that I am a woman – I just am – but it impacts on every single thing that I do and how others perceive me. The same goes for being a feminist. I am a feminist because in so many things I do there is some form of inequality caused by being a woman, whether it is walking down the street alone at night or the bill being presented to the man in a restaurant. Obviously some of these are less worrying than others – I'm delighted if somebody wants to buy me dinner – but I certainly don't want that decision to be made on my behalf.

Some people say we have equality now, so who needs feminism? Presumably they don't mind that women get paid on average just eighty-three per cent of men's salaries; in effect we get paid until the end of October, then work the rest of the year for nothing. These might be the same women who do all the washing in their household because it is easier to put everything in together, and then find it strange that men just assume washing and cleaning is women's work.

When I asked my friends whether they are feminists, many reacted with horror. They assumed that if they said yes, they could not also be feminine, they could not shave their legs and they would have to hate men. There was a sense that saying yes meant no more short skirts and no more make-up, that it would mean they had to vote in a particular way or have specific interests and that to say they were a feminist would make them part of a specific political movement that they were not comfortable with.

None of this is the case, at least not in noughties feminism. Yet even I sometimes feel uneasy about feminism. My husband has a badge that he picked up from the Fawcett Society, an organisation that promotes equality between men and women. It says 'real men are feminists'. I love him for having it – maybe that's why he got it in the first place – but I'd probably be embarrassed if he wore it in public. After all, feminism can be an embarrassing word. The term seems to make most people think of bra burning and hairy armpits which is a shame because while 1970s feminists achieved a lot that women today should be grateful for, they are not the only icons of the feminist movement. I have no intention of ever throwing myself in front of a horse, very little makes me want to chain myself to the railings at Downing Street and my longest hunger strike has been about an hour, but the suffragettes are my feminist icons. What's more, I am a feminist who wears a bra and shaves my armpits. I don't see it as a choice between being feminine and being feminist.

Nor do I necessarily need to know my place in feminist history. You don't need to know what steps we have made towards equality – you just need to know that we're not there yet. We're campaigning to be equal, not less unequal.

When I am asked about feminism and someone brings up the name of a once famous but now long forgotten feminist, I often feel rather stupid when I confess I haven't heard of her. So when I wrote an article for the *Guardian* newspaper about men who ask their girlfriend's dad for permission to marry them and my editor rang me and said 'It's great, but can you add a quote from a second wave feminist' I just bluffed and said 'Of course.' And then as soon as I put the phone down I called my mum. 'What's a second wave feminist?' I asked. She wasn't entirely sure what my editor meant either.

So I did what any self-respecting journalist would do, and googled it. The results threw up a list on *Wikipedia*, a website I tell the journalism students I teach never to rely on. It said:

Second Wave Feminism is generally identified with a period beginning in the early 1960s. The movement encouraged women to understand aspects of their own personal lives as deeply politicized, and reflective of a sexist structure of power. If first-wave feminism focused upon absolute rights such as suffrage, second-wave feminism was largely concerned with other issues of equality, such as the end to discrimination and oppression.

Wikipedia then named sixty-six second wave feminists. I had heard of six, one of whom was Oprah Winfrey, who I had associated with black rights and fat rights but not feminism. I knew what another, Andrea Dworkin, had looked like but not what she stood for. Germaine Greer had become something of a rent-a-gob in the UK, and a stereotypical man-hating feminist. I had heard of Gloria Steinem and Beatrix Campbell somewhere in the dark recesses of my brain but couldn't tell you why. I called the other one I had heard of, Hilary Wainwright. I knew her because she edited a political magazine, *Red Pepper,* not because of her feminism. We had a great chat and she helped me with the article, enlisting her mum, Joyce, eighty-five at the time, who was with her when I phoned. Joyce told us about a poem that girls used to say when she was a child. It suggested that using your dad as an excuse not to marry was a feminist gesture, telling the suitor to go to hell. It went:

Go to father she said,
When he asked her to wed,
Though she knew that he knew,

That her father was dead.
And she knew that he knew,
What a life he had led,
And she knew that he knew,
What she meant when she said, Go to father.

At the end of our chat I asked Hilary if she was a second wave feminist. 'I'm not sure' she said. So much for *Wikipedia*. And so much for feminist history, when even the big names don't know if they are part of a specific movement or not.

So this book isn't about our place as noughties women in the history of feminism. It isn't about looking back at women's place and congratulating society on how far we've come. It's not about knowing your Naomi Wolf from your Virginia Woolf or your Guerrilla Girls from your Spice Girls.

Instead this book will take you on a journey through various aspects of a noughtie girl's life to persuade you that feminism is a real issue for today's women and not just an embarrassing word. And what do I mean by noughtie girl? Well in the broadest sense, noughtie girls are any women alive in the noughties, the first decade of the twenty-first century. But specifically, women born in the seventies, eighties, nineties and noughties are the generation of women I am referring to as noughtie girls. Women who were children or not even born when the UK had its first female Prime Minister, women who have always known they could access legal abortion should they want it, women whose mothers could have taken the contraceptive pill.

This book is about noughtie girls but it is not just for them. It is for their mums, sisters, aunts and grandparents. And of course for their partners, dads, brothers, uncles, grandfathers and friends. For it is a window into some of the areas noughtie girls need to think about in their lives, whether they are asking themselves who to sleep with, whether to apply for promotion or why the art gallery they are in has no paintings by women artists.

A note however on women who are lesbians. Sexuality is often lumped in with other gender issues, in bookshops and on university courses at least. In part this is because the two issues became bound together in previous incarnations of feminism, where having sex with men was seen as betraying the sisterhood and lesbianism was as much a political statement as an expression of your true sexuality. This is not the case among noughtie girls, who tend to see lesbianism as an instinctive sexuality rather than as a political choice. But as I have no direct experience of many of the issues specifically concerning lesbians I have not attempted to cover these here. Therefore the chapters on sex and on marriage are about heterosexual relationships. Other than that however I hope that this book is interesting for all women.

Being a feminist is what you want it to be. For me, it's about having real choices and demanding equality. We all make different choices; I want the choice to decide who I go out with, who I sleep with, who I marry and if I divorce. I want to choose my own surname and my own title. I want to choose who runs my country. I want to choose when I conceive and, if I do conceive by accident, I want to choose whether I have an abortion or whether I keep the child. If I do have children, I want to choose whether I look after them or whether somebody else does. I want to choose whether I wear high heels or flat shoes, whether I wear trousers or skirts, whether I wear make-up and yes, whether I wear a bra. If I want to roller skate down the promenade wearing white jeans while on my period as that famous tampon advert had it, I will, and if I want to take to bed with a hot water bottle and the DVD box set of *Sex and the City*, I'll do that instead. I want to choose whether to go to university, whether to work in an office or at home and whether to accept a job or not. I want to choose whether I cook, whether I clean and whether I do the laundry.

And I want equality. I want equal pay with men. I want equal opportunities for education, jobs, sport and entertainment. I want equality when it comes to responsibility for caring for the vulnerable in society, be it our children or our elderly parents. I want equality of moral rhetoric so promiscuity amongst women is not seen as worse than promiscuity amongst men, so teenage girls who binge drink are no worse than teenage boys. And I want equality of expectation, so boys and girls are all expected to be the best people they can.

Once we have these choices and equality, frankly I don't care what other women do with it. If they want to get married, take their husband's surname, look after their children, cook, wash and clean for their family and take the kids to school every day, then so be it. As long as they believe that everybody has the right to choose whether or not to do these things, then they are feminists too.

1

The sisterhood

First things first – what is this idea of sisterhood that feminists refer to? The sisterhood refers to the idea that we have something in common with other women just because we are women and that because of this bond we have an obligation to help each other.

In some respects this is true – as women we all face certain stereotyping and prejudices, and there are many issues in which all women have a stake. But sisterhood is complicated. After all, we all live contradictory lives to some extent. One woman I know is to all intents and purposes a leading member of the sisterhood. She buys her daughter toy cars and blue clothes as she is adamant she won't grow up forced into gender stereotypes. She is active in women's groups and works hard to educate her friends about women's issues. Yet she is also the woman I think is most likely to try to sleep with my husband.

So what should sisterhood mean to a noughtie girl? Well it doesn't mean that we have to like all women. It doesn't mean that every woman is nice, or deserves our friendship. Women can be stupid, they can be vindictive and they can be shits. But sisterhood means judging people for how they act, not just because they are a woman, and applying the same standards to determining whether they are stupid, vindictive or shits as we would to men. It also means not judging other women by different standards to those we judge men by, not calling other women sluts and not slagging off the way they look or the choices they make.

And sisterhood also means that we are a movement that is greater than the sum of its parts, made up of women who may not agree with each other on every subject, but who have the same basic demands. So if you believe that women should have equality and that women should have choices you are part of the sisterhood, which is basically just another way of saying you are a woman who wants things to be better for all women.

Who are noughtie girls and what do we believe?
One of the reasons people deny being a feminist is not that they don't necessarily believe in the feminist cause, but because they worry that if they are asked whether they are a feminist and say yes, they will then be asked precisely what they mean by that, and struggle to come up with an answer

To be proud of being a feminist, and to persuade others that it's not a woolly position to take, all noughtie girls should work out a short definition of feminism that works for them, preferably something your nice but slightly thick mate would also understand if you explained it to them.

Every feminist's definition is different of course, as it should be – we're a collection of people with the same values, not one person. But here is mine:

Feminism is about believing that no one should be treated differently, judged differently, afforded different rights or forced into specific roles in society according to their sex.

You could change the last word from sex to race, class, sexuality or age if you wanted and have an equally good definition of not being racist, classist, homophobic or ageist.

So according to my definition, if you decide that caring roles are only women's work then you are not a feminist. If you think it's okay to pay men and women different amounts for doing the same job then you are not a feminist. If you think women should look and act in a certain way then you are not a feminist. And if you have different standards of behaviour for men and women then you are not a feminist.

Other people define feminism differently. I like this from Holly Combe on *The F Word* website:

Does your enjoyment of a book tend to be somewhat hampered if its references to the general reader or subject constantly default to the pronoun 'he'? If so, you're probably a feminist.

Introducing Feminism by Susan Alice Watkins, Marisa Rueda and Marta Rodriguez offers a more traditional definition:

Feminism is about challenging the division of labour in the world that puts men in charge of the public sphere — work, sports, wars, government — while women slave away unpaid in the home, carrying the whole burden of family life.

All three definitions show that we have moved on somewhat from basic demands for women such as the right to have an education, to vote or to work and to keep their own earnings.

Introducing Feminism also looks at the way the women's movement has typically been split into three groups: radical feminists, socialist feminists and liberal feminists. Radical feminists feel that the problem is patriarchy — living in a society in which the whole system is set up so that men have power over women. Socialist feminists see male domination as being mixed up with class exploitation, with the answer being to not just get more rights for women but to fight against capitalism as well. Liberal feminists focus more on equal rights legislation and pro-women reforms.

Noughtie girls do not split along these lines. Our demands are less based on political ideologies and more based on the experiences we have in our day-to-day lives. But if you wanted to categorise the types of women who make up noughtie girl feminists then you could probably split them into the following four categories:

1. *Louds and prouds* are the women who immediately acknowledge that they are feminist. They probably make public statements about their feminism such as

4

insisting on being called Ms, keeping their surname if they get married and being actively involved in specific causes. They are the first to challenge sexist assumptions and they are happy to let anyone who wants to know, and anyone who doesn't, that feminism is a key part of their outlook on life.

2. *Unintentional feminists* are people who don't necessarily even think about feminism, but they instinctively act in a way that feminists would hope someone would act. So they hold a door open whether for a man or a woman, they buy bar staff a drink not because they fancy them but because they have done a good job, they ask women what title they like rather than make an assumption, they never walk into a room of several women and one man and assume the man is in charge. Being an unintentional feminist is really just a synonym for good manners.

3. *Accidental feminists* don't necessarily set out to identify themselves as feminists. But then something happens to them – they are passed over for promotion at work in favour of a man, or they realise they are earning less than men doing the same job, or they don't feel safe walking home, or they get looked through by the sales-person when trying to buy a car, and this makes them angry. They might not think of themselves as political animals, but they do think of themselves as human beings of equal worth, and their own experience makes them stand up for equality.

4. *Feminisn'ts* are the women who, when talking about women's rights or their own beliefs, start a sentence with 'I'm not a feminist but ...' and then go on to state their beliefs, all of which tally with the causes of feminism. Like, 'I'm not a feminist but I do believe men and women doing the same job should be paid the same' or 'I'm not a feminist but I think men should do their share of the housework.' It is, it seems, the word they dislike not the concepts. I would rather feminisn'ts became feminists, but having a set of beliefs that are similar to those that we call feminism is good enough for me whatever they call it.

Whichever type you are – loud and proud, unintentional, accidental or feminisn't – noughtie girl feminism has room for you all. And though we may all come up with a different definition of what we mean by feminist, I am sure we'll all like this quotation from the author Rebecca West:

> *I myself have never been able to find out precisely what feminism is: I only know that people call me a feminist whenever I express sentiments that differentiate me from a door mat or a prostitute.*

What about foreign women?
This book is concerned with the lives of women in the developed West. Compared to women elsewhere in the world, we have fantastically free lives, though this should not be used as

an argument to stop us getting complete equality in the West of course.

But as feminists is it essential that we are aware of and attempt to change the lot of women elsewhere in the world? Should there be a sense of international sisterhood? For example, should we be annoyed that in Swaziland married women are legal minors unless otherwise stated in their pre-nup, or that in the Democratic Republic of Congo women need their husband's permission to open a bank account, or that in Yemen a woman cannot leave the house without her husband's consent, or that in Saudi Arabia women cannot drive cars or ride bicycles, or that in Syria a man can ask the government to prevent his wife leaving the country.

Ruthie Samuel wrote about the lack of interest in international women's rights in an article for *The F Word* website. She argues that by focusing on the smaller issues at home women in the Western world ignore international sisterhood and laments the lack of attention we give women's rights abroad:

> *We're talking about fifty per cent of these populations being denied basic rights, abused, disdained and patronised and yet you wouldn't know it from the lack of attention paid to these issues by our media, society and politicians ... This is why UK feminists can't afford to get distracted by debating what we should be wearing and whether or not it matters if we choose to work part time. We need to focus on getting these [international] human rights abuses the attention they deserve.*

7

Whilst I agree with Samuel that we need to condemn human rights abuses abroad loudly and clearly, she is wrong that we can't do this at the same time as fighting for the smaller issues in the UK. Part of the essence of being a noughtie girl is to question the world around us. But it's also to ensure that we question inequality in all its forms. Our battles in our society may not be as fundamental as the battles of women in some other countries around the world, but they are still battles that need fighting. We can apply the sisterhood on two levels – both the need to improve women's lives around the world at a human rights level, and the push for greater equality in our own lives, and while this book focuses on the second of these, it does not mean we should ignore the importance of the first.

A girl's best friends

Love it or hate it, and I loved it, the television show *Sex and the City* did help explain to the world just how important female friendships are to noughties women. For to understand noughtie girls properly you first have to understand the nature of female friendship.

Perhaps it's because we don't live in the same street as our parents any more, or because we stay single for longer, but our friends are the ones we rely on most of all. Our female friends are the people we turn to when we are worried about a job interview, the people whose shoulders we cry on when our hearts are broken, when we are excited about a date, when we need wardrobe advice, when we need an abortion. They are the people we tell our secrets to.

Yet despite this, sometimes we don't even like our female friends. Certainly female friendship isn't the nurturing, stable, supportive bubble some people might think it looks like. Within friendship circles there are constant battles going on for the alpha female position. We are delighted when someone's relationship is going well, but sometimes we secretly prefer the joy of hearing about it when it has gone wrong. We bitch behind each other's backs, and can be incredibly two faced. Nevertheless, female friendship is the essence of most noughtie girls' lives because it is the most stable thing we have. Relationships may come and go, families may have other underlying tensions, colleagues may move on, but our friends will always take our calls and will always make sympathetic noises, even if they slag us off later without us knowing. In one sense our friends are the only certain thing in our uncertain world.

Such single sex friendship groups with such importance placed upon them are rather new, perhaps the consequence of settling down later and so not being monopolised by a partner or caught up in the drudgery of looking after the home and children too early. Certainly to have this kind of friendship you also need financial freedom so you can spend your own money on going out. And perhaps they are the consequence of marriage no longer being the most important thing in society, so that now we're no longer fighting each other for men, or competing to find a husband, we instead need people to go out and have fun with. Though fun is not just equated with sex, essentially this means going to bars and clubs to look for sex, or at the very least male attention, and going out for meals and shopping together and examining where things went right or wrong. I am not saying that women are only concerned with finding a mate, and that we can't also talk about literature, the arts, sport etc, and there isn't the urgency there once was, but finding a mate is a huge part of female friendships. By the time we do find our partners, we're so reliant on our female friends that they are fixtures in our lives, plus we need them to talk to about our partner and to get reassurance that we are normal.

Perhaps this is why men often feel threatened by groups of female friends, resorting to calling female-only groups lesbians, or covens, as if we must be either sexually attracted to each other or witches to wish to spend time without the menfolk.

But perhaps the main reason we need female friends is because we can truly be ourselves with them. My friends and I have an all female book group. Occasionally men have wanted to join us but we have always said no. In part this is because we don't only talk about the book, but also about our love lives, our careers, our recent shopping expeditions. But it is also because with only one sex present, we no longer conform to gender stereotypes. We can be forceful in our opinions, or we can keep them to ourselves. We can admit we don't understand something without it being because we are a woman, and we can draw parallels with other books without being worried we are being too clever. By defining our club by our sex, we lose the gender stereotypes once we are in it, and instead of being women, we are just people.

Crying she-wolf, or how to recognise discrimination

We need to be aware that things might happen to women that are unfair but are not necessarily a result of sexism. Yes sure, you could make the argument that living in a patriarchal society everything is the product of keeping men up and women down and is therefore inherently sexist, but beyond rising up and killing all men, what can we do?

We can't call everything that doesn't go right for women sexist. Is war anti-women? Well actually it's anti-human. Where there is a panel of three at a conference session and they are all men is that sexism? It might be, or it may be that in that instance the three most suitable speakers were men. A man gets given the job? Perhaps he was the best candidate. Similarly we mustn't assume that every time we see a cleaner and it is a woman, it is a case of discrimination. (It is also possible that the person in question is facing another form of discrimination – class, age, sexuality, disability or race for example.)

I think we're lucky that we're in a position now where institutional sexism at least is largely viewed as unacceptable. To maintain this, and to stop sexism wherever it occurs, we need to name and shame perpetrators and make a fuss where it is happening. But we must also be careful not to shoot ourselves in our collective foot, and call everything that isn't how we want it to be sexist, or we undermine our demands.

How I learnt to stop worrying and love Posh Spice

Despite the fact that sisterhood is about not judging other women, I bet most of us do it a lot of the time. How many of us can open a celebrity magazine and, looking at the women pictured, not judge them in some way? There are those that we think would be our best friends if only we lived next door to them. Then there are those that we think are too fat, too thin, too tarty or not talented. Therefore the following opinion may upset some of you but I am going to write it loudly and proudly. I like Victoria Beckham. I don't know her personally of course, I have no idea whether she is nice to her friends, encouraging to her children and loving to her husband, but as much as I can know about her through reading magazines and newspapers, I like.

So I was quite surprised when some years ago watching a football match on telly in a pub, the cameras panned round the stadium and settled on Victoria, watching the game in which David Beckham was playing. Nearly the whole pub, both men and women, booed at the sight of her.

As far as I'm concerned Victoria should be a feminist icon. As a Spice Girl and instrumental in the girl power phenomenon, she was part of one of the most successful female businesses in history. They made a fortune and even fired their male manager to run their own affairs. She both makes the most of her looks and doesn't hide away when she has a bout of acne. What's more, she even got her man to wear a skirt in public.

And what about the non-feminists, the people who find this kind of thing threatening? Well they should like her too, for in other ways Victoria is the opposite of feminist thought. After all, she's always perfectly turned out, she changed her name upon marriage and more or less gave up her own career to produce three male heirs. Surely this is the image many men have of an ideal wife.

The novelist Fay Weldon calls herself a feminist yet she provides one of the worst examples of hatred towards Victoria and the rest of the Spice Girls, writing in the *Daily Mail* in December 2007 with her reaction to their reunion tour:

> *Forgive me for being blunt, but if a generation of our young womanhood has taken to binge drinking, Saturday night sluttishness and 'happy-slappings', I blame the Spice Girls ... Though some will no doubt disagree, and argue that the Spice Girls are simply a slice of bubblegum pop history, I believe the aspirations and attitudes of these five women go hand-in-hand with the decline of our culture over the past decade.*

It turns out though, later on in her article, that what bothers Weldon most of all is that these girls not only grew up but they continued, post children, to work and to have their own identities.

> *Now they're on tour again, soaring above the world in their specially chartered Boeing 747, along with their crèches and their entourage. But this time around the image they project is obviously and entirely contrived, with all that youthful zest replaced by weary cynicism. The difference between those five*

13

breezily-sexual, energetic, bouncy girls singing about Girl Power ten years back and the five sugar-coated, air-brushed, painfully-thin, desperate mums-on-tour is clear to see. Sexy strip-teases, I ask you! Of the five of them, two are married (one of those for the second time and not to the father of her baby), one is a single mother, and two have long-term partners.

It seems to me that the Spice Girls found the perfect answer to being working mothers, taking their children to the work crèche is something that most working parents would love to have the opportunity to do. Does Weldon really believe that women, once they have children or settle down with a partner, are not allowed to be sexy any more, to have their own interests and to juggle their home lives with their working lives? I doubt it.

No, what Weldon objects to isn't the Spice Girls, it's working mothers and women taking charge of their own sexiness and using it as they wish and to please themselves and other women (the majority of their audience), rather than for men. Weldon may call herself a feminist but in this article at least she's just a misogynist in feminist clothing, and so are the women who claim to dislike Victoria Beckham for being a disgrace to women.

My Cherie Amour

If I haven't put you off with my liking of Victoria Beckham, then I probably will with this defence of Cherie Blair. She's old news now but for the end of the nineties and first half of the noughties the woman everybody loved to hate was Cherie Blair, the wife of the then Prime Minister Tony Blair. And though they hated Cherie Blair a lot, they hated her alter ego, Cherie Booth (her maiden name), the successful QC, even more.

What is it that made women hate Cherie so? I don't buy the argument that she was an inherently unlikable person, or that as the public grew more disenchanted with the Government they liked everyone associated with it less. I think the answer is much more misogynistic than that, and due to a perhaps unconscious dislike of clever women or women who have power.

With Cherie, people seemed to think she was pulling some of the strings when it came to the Prime Minister making decisions – people thought she had his ear. In fact, as a political animal herself, as an intelligent woman in Downing Street and as his wife, she probably did. This is in contrast to the public perception of Margaret Thatcher's husband Denis, or John Major's wife Norma, both of whom were seen but not heard.

People also hated the idea that Cherie wasn't a dumpy little housewife. She was in fact the woman who had it all. She had lots of kids, a high powered job and a successful husband. In the public's dislike of her there was a sense of 'you can't have it all matey'. Hence there were lots of stories about her not being a good lawyer, or not looking after her children properly or neglecting her image. Yet even when Cherie did sort out her image she received hatred for this. The fact was, Cherie was never going to be most people's ideal woman because their ideal woman is not someone with brains and a job.

This isn't always the case for high profile female partners of male politicians. Compare the press's treatment of Cherie with the reception Carla Bruni, married to Nicholas Sarkozy, President of France, got when she came to London in 2008 – there was an almost universal swooning. Yes, Bruni is a former supermodel, but she is also recognised as being immensely influential on her husband, yet no one accused her of wielding power with the same venom they did Cherie.

There seems to be a double standard here. If a beautiful woman with a career in modelling or something 'feminine' then shows that she has brains and goes into politics (or humanitarian work or film directing or other high profile but demanding roles) everyone says how amazing they are. If on the other hand an intelligent woman with a high profile career suddenly becomes elegant or beautiful, then they are derided for trying too hard and seen as being greedy. People explain this away in lots of ways. In Australia it is called tall poppy syndrome, the idea being that the tallest poppies are the ones that are cut down. In the UK we see it as bringing people back down to earth, or stopping them getting too big for their boots. But the truth is, it's misogyny.

Stealing men

Even when we don't want to be with someone, it's amazing how protective we can be over them. I have no desire whatsoever to be back with a man I dated in my early twenties, but I do rather hate the fact that he had a new partner and a child before me. As a friend of mine said: 'It hurts when they do something before you, that's why it's called the human race.'

Part of being a noughtie girl is recognising that we are all responsible for our own actions. That's why when we talk about women trying to steal men away (or the other way round) we get it so wrong. We don't have ownership over people, therefore no one can be stolen. When somebody chooses to leave his or her partner for another, or has an affair, that person is totally complicit in this.

But although this may be fine in principle, it can be hard to accept in practice. Three women I know used to work in the same office. The first woman split up with her partner and found another. The second woman went out with the first partner of the first woman for a while. The third one went out with another man who later on ended up going out with the ex-partner of the first women's new partner. Confused? We certainly were. But for a while at least it seemed like the perfect example of noughties relationships in which we try people out until we find the right one, and in which we accept our ex-partners have new lives to the point where we even accept that this may be with our friends.

But that's not often the case in real life. For though we all thought how very grown up everyone had been, how accepting we were of people having to make their own decisions and about relationships not always working out, how we were grown-up members of the sisterhood, we are all still extremely wary of the new partner of the first woman's first partner.

That's the thing about sisterhood – even for the most feminist of noughtie girls when it's your friends who are hurt the sisterhood takes a back seat and standing by your friends takes precedence.

Do feminists hate men?

There's a great picture by the feminist cartoonist Jacky Fleming which shows two women having a chat. One woman says:

> ... *then he said why was I always trying to change him and I said probably because he's such an obnoxious thoughtless selfish overbearing self-righteous hypocritical arrogant loudmouthed misogynist bastard ...*

Seeing cartoons such as this, and book titles such as *Are Men Necessary?* by Maureen Dowd, my edition of which is illustrated rather starkly with two walnuts placed to look like testicles on the front cover, it would be reasonable for men to ask 'do feminists hate men?' After all, even in children's musicals women are rather disparaging of their menfolk – in *Mary Poppins* (the film, not the stage version) Mrs Bank's sings *Sister Suffragette* and walks around with a 'Votes for Women' sash and proclaims:

> *We're clearly soldiers in petticoats*
> *And dauntless crusaders for woman's votes*
> *Though we adore men individually*
> *We agree that as a group they're rather stupid!*

Not so different from the quotation from Nancy Astor, the first woman to take her seat in the House of Commons: 'I married beneath me – all women do.'

But of course noughtie girls don't hate men. Nor do we think all, or even most, men are misogynist or women haters. What feminists hate is the way society works so that women have fewer choices in their lives than men do. Men should hate their lack of choice too. Other than a very few men, how many really can afford to work flexibly to see more of their children? How many can enter typically female professions without encountering sexism? Think how quick people are to assume that male primary school teachers are gay.

But if men are also treated unfairly by society, shouldn't they have a movement of their own? I sometimes wonder what a modern day men's movement might look like, if men were to organise and campaign for equal rights.

A men's movement would definitely campaign for better paternity leave and the right to flexible working. They would look at access to children for men separated from their children's mothers. They might focus on illnesses that affect men – male infertility, prostate cancer etc. And perhaps there would be an attempt to stop jokes based on penis size. They would campaign to end advertising that showed men bulging out of their underpants, making ordinary men feel inadequate. They would appeal to women not to be scared when they are walking behind them on a dark street. Their posters might have slogans such as 'I'm a man not a rapist'. They would draw attention to the statistics that show one in six men will be the victim of domestic violence during their lifetime.

A man's movement like this would not be a bad thing. Whether it is necessary however is debatable, for all those things are effectively achieved through the women's movement. We want men to take an active role in looking after their children and we want working practices to be such that men can take extended paternity leave just as women do. We don't want to assume that the main breadwinner in the family will automatically be the man. We want men to live long and healthy lives and to not feel inadequate. We don't want to feel afraid of men when we walk down the street. Therefore feminism is a men's movement as well as a women's movement, which is why all men should also consider themselves feminist.

The invisible woman

Some women I know tell me that they feel they have become invisible, not just to men but to women too. This is particularly the case with middle aged women – no longer deemed sexually attractive and no longer fertile, they are literally looked through by other people when trying to buy a drink, when applying for jobs or when just walking down the street.

Linda, a friend of mine in her forties, married with two children, says she feels invisible all the time.

I often think I am invisible. At my kids' school I am referred to either by my partner's name or as my children's mum. It's not that I don't love being these things, but I am a person in my own right too.

Another woman says the same:

I am always seen as someone's partner or mum, or just another scruffy overweight lady standing at the school gates or scowling in the supermarket. I've gone from being called 'love' (which I really don't mind) to 'madam' which I hate. And worse, to doctor's receptionists, schoolteachers and even cold bloody callers, I'm referred to by my partner's surname when we're not even married.

Other women tell me of being in queues at restaurants waiting to be served and just being ignored as if they are not there. But it's not just men doing this that they complain about, but women too.

Perhaps one of the worst things about this invisibility is that women realise they have effectively always been invisible except for their desirability. What they thought was attention in their youth proves to be nothing much more than sexual interest or desire anyway. Women may have fooled themselves into thinking that it was their personality people liked, but the truth is interesting people rarely become boring and wits rarely lose their humour, so if the attention has tailed off then it is unlikely to be that. No, the sad truth is that the attention wasn't often based on the being interesting or being humorous in the first place.

Hopefully one of the good things that will come out of being a young feminist in the noughties will be that we have identities separate to that of our partners or our children and that the way we view ourselves is far less centred on beauty than in the past. Perhaps we need to have the confidence that noughtie girls have and that we have gained only through the feminist advances made by previous generations to be able to demand attention in our own right when we are middle aged women ourselves, something that will be helped by our financial independence that means businesses will not be able to afford to ignore us.

But in the meantime it seems to me that a vital part of the sisterhood is ensuring women are not ignored, either by men or by other women. This is easier said than done – after all, if you are under thirty-five and reading this ask yourself when you last spoke to a woman twenty years older than you who is not a relative or one of their friends, or a colleague or someone in the service industry?

At the moment, for women who are over a certain age, it seems like a case of the poem *I met a man who wasn't there*, though here I have changed the subject's sex:

As I was walking up the stair,
I met a woman who wasn't there.
She wasn't there again today,
I wish that woman would go away.

Middle aged women may not be seen as exciting, though some

are of course. They may not be thought of as sexually attractive or even sexually active, though many are. They may not shout the loudest or spend the most. But if noughtie girls are to have any hope for visibility as they age, we must start noticing the middle aged women currently around us.

2

Language

You've probably heard about some feminists' attempts to make language more equal. Why should 'women' be derivative of 'men', they argue, opting instead for 'womyn' or 'wimmin'. History is about men, but what about 'herstory' they may say. These words may make a point but they don't necessarily do feminism any favours, attracting ridicule and a rolling of eyes more than an understanding of equality.

I have never used an alternative spelling of 'women' – I think it would undermine my feminist arguments by making people laugh rather than take my arguments seriously and besides, I am in favour of a uniformity of spelling across a language. But language does matter. Words we choose to use every day often tell their own story of sexism, from the words policeman and fireman which help convey the idea that these jobs should be done by men (we should use police officer and firefighter), to the double standards that Jessica Valenti exposes so well in her book *He's a Stud, She's a Slut, and 49 Other Double Standards Every Woman Should Know*, which not only looks at the different ways we judge men and women, but at the language used to do so.

We each have our own bugbears about language. Mine are being called by the masculine version of a job title where a unisex word would do just as well – chairman instead of chair for example – and my title which has always been, currently is and always will be Ms. Other women will have their own non-negotiable areas. It doesn't so much matter what each woman gets concerned about when it comes to language, but it does matter that she realises the strength of language when it comes to undermining equality, and chooses the words that she uses, and that she lets others use, wisely.

Sheedom fighters and other suggestions

While most women don't have a problem with the concepts that we associate with feminism, many dislike the word. 'I'm not a feminist' is said with as much vehemence as 'I'm not a paedophile' or 'I'm not racist.'

So what is it about the word feminist that puts people off? At a talk I went to in the summer of 2006 in New York, the feminist journalist Ariel Levy was in conversation with the feminist writer Erica Jong. 'What should I say to my friends who believe in equality but hate the word feminist?' I asked them. Ariel Levy replied: 'Tell them to find another way to rebel against their mothers.' But it's not just a case of rebelling against our mothers – that might be true for the daughters of self-proclaimed feminists but lots of our mothers also dislike the word feminism.

Perhaps this is because the word feminist has become too associated with a particular type of feminism, one where people think they need to be angry all the time, where they need to look and speak a certain way. Feminism, they say, has become synonymous with the worst aspects of the women's movement.

I did a straw poll of friends, both feminists and non-feminists, and the only alternatives to 'feminist' which came up were variants on the word equal. Equalitist however suggests a concern with discrimination against all types of social group – age, sexuality and race as well as gender. Now I'm not saying this shouldn't be the case, and feminists should be aware of and opposed to discrimination on all levels, but feminism expressly recognises that women are not equal in society because they are women. If we bind it up with other forms of discrimination then we lose sight of the specific fight for women's equality.

I came up with a couple of words as alternatives for feminism but both sound like bad catchphrases designed to get your attention on a magazine cover rather than serious names for a set of beliefs, particularly my first attempt – Sheedom Fighters.

Nu-feminism was the other one, building on Natasha Walter's new feminists that she wrote about in 1997 in *The New Feminism* and playing on the idea that we have reinvented many movements from nu-rave music to New Labour, but perhaps for these connotations alone it is more exclusive than inclusive. The same goes for neo-feminism.

But does the word matter at all? If someone thinks like a feminist and acts like a feminist, does it matter if they call themselves a feminist?

I think the answer is yes. If we unite under one word, if everyone who believes in equality of opportunity and choices for women calls themselves one name and boldly states that they are this one name, then we cannot be ignored, accused of factionalism or dismissed as a fringe movement. One woman standing alone may achieve change in her own life, she may achieve some changes for other women, but she is not as strong as an army of women standing as one and demanding change.

Plus when we deny we are something we take on the air of being embarrassed or ashamed. I am not ashamed or apologetic to be a feminist and neither should you be.

Please call me Ms E Levenson

Since as long as I have had control over how I am addressed, I have been a Ms. I am not a Miss and whatever my marital status, I have no intention of ever being a Mrs.

Many people, men and women, have asked me why this is and the answer is a very simple one. Unless you are trying to pick me up, at no point should my marital status have any impact on how you treat me, therefore, you have no need to know it.

Some friends of mine have been keen to use Miss, thinking that it makes them seem younger than they are. Why any grown woman would want to give the impression of being a prepubescent girl is beyond me. I can't imagine an adult man in any situation outside of sado-masochism saying 'Call me Master.' No, all men post puberty are Mr.

One of my banks sends me letters addressed to Miss Levenson. Every time I spend money I get annoyed (unfortunately that doesn't stop me spending it), but when I get these letters it's particularly annoying. It's only the bureaucracy involved that stops me bothering to change it to Ms. When I have to talk to officials on the phone and I am asked my title, I always say Ms and correct people when they refer to me as Miss, and while I wouldn't go so far as to say that I am sure the person at the other end of the phone is passing notes to their mates saying 'We've got a feminist on line one', it is definitely possible to sense an eyebrow being raised over the phone.

Although I am a Ms, I don't actually see the point of having a title at all. It should, after all, only be necessary to know whether a person you have not yet met is a man or a woman when deciding whether to invite them to a smear test or other medical interventions.

I am, despite being married, not only a definite Ms, but I have also kept the surname I was given at birth – Levenson.

I made the issue of my name crystal clear in the speech I gave when I got married. I intended our guests to go away knowing in no uncertain terms how to address letters to me. In between the thank yous and the part about why I love my husband, I said:

Richard and I have thought carefully about surnames. We decided pretty quickly that Richard and Ellie Levenson-Messingham was too much of a mouthful. We rejected Richard and Ellie Messyson, and Ellie and Richard Levingham, and Richard categorically refused to consider adopting my favourite flower and becoming Ellie and Richard Daffodil. Likewise he rejected all the pretty names I suggested including Ellie and Richard Friend, Ellie and Richard Jolly, Ellie and Richard Valentine, Ellie and Richard Vine and Ellie and Richard Fluffy. So we remain Mr Richard Messingham and Ms Ellie Levenson, a marriage of two feminists, and we vow to return unopened any post referring to us as Mr and Mrs Ellie Levenson.

There was a spontaneous burst of applause from some of my more feminist friends who got this final joke and I hoped this would be the end of the matter.

Yet almost immediately I started to get post from some people who had heard the speech addressed to Mrs R Messingham. I was annoyed that people hadn't listened properly to my categorical rejection of both of these constituent parts of the name, but I knew it would happen. What I hadn't prepared for was being referred to by Richard's initial. Mrs Messingham might just, at a stretch, and especially if there was a cheque

29

inside, be me. But Mrs R Messingham? Why on earth would I have taken on Richard's initial as well?

Sometimes I imagine me and Richard explaining our names to our future children (surnames yet to be decided). I will tell them the following, like a fairy story:

> One day two people met. They were separate people with separate lives but they liked each other very much. They wanted to find a way to be together but they wanted to remain themselves. Ellie wanted to stay Ellie and Richard wanted to stay Richard. Neither of them wanted to change their name to Rillie or Elichard...

'Rillie or Elichard,' they might exclaim, 'what silly names.'

> ... and yes, they are silly, particularly because Ellie thinks of herself as Ellie and Richard thinks of himself as Richard. Ellie is like a stick of rock you might buy at the seaside – if you chopped her up you would find Ellie written through her all the way. Richard is the same. Any other name would feel wrong to them.
>
> So Ellie and Richard rejected Rillie and Elichard and for similar reasons they rejected combining their surnames. Instead they lived happily ever after with their own names, as individuals who just happen to be married.

Sometimes I think about those people who change their names, and how much they must hate themselves, their families and their identities up until this point to want to destroy their identity and leave their name behind.

Some people however say it is the other way round. I know people who have taken the surname of their husband upon marriage because, they say, it shows just how much they love him that they want to bear his name.

Do I not love my husband enough to take his name? I thought about it. No, I concluded, it's not that I don't love my husband enough to take his name, it's that I love myself enough not to.

Complaint letter

Dear festival admin team,

I am trying to book tickets to your arts festival this summer and tried to book online. I was saddened to see your online registration form only allowed people to choose Miss, Mrs, Mr or Dr as their title. As a Ms, I am neither Miss nor Mrs, so chose Dr as I am more likely to be that in the future than change into a man, although at this moment I am neither.

Would it be possible to add a Ms option to your online registration form as marital status does not have an impact on which shows people would like to see?

Kind regards,

Ellie Levenson

The cock and cunt

The cock and cunt. It sounds like a rather nice country pub with a fire crackling in the hearth and a Sunday roast on the menu.

Alas, there's no such pub called this that I know of, but the words are often used in my household. I often call my husband a cock. It is a term of endearment really, or so I tell him. You know, as in he steals the duvet when it's cold and I call him a cock. We return home both needing a pee and he gets to the bathroom first so I call him a cock. Nothing out of the ordinary. Then one day I called him a cock and he turned round to verbally retaliate and decided to call me a cunt.

Cunt. Some people have been shocked when I tell them this is something I am regularly called. The word is one of the worst swear words in our language. I too was surprised at first. But now, after due consideration, I find it rather funny. It is one of our in-jokes I suppose. I call him a cock. He calls me a cunt. The only way it doesn't work is that usually when I call him a cock he is acting in a manner to deserve this and when he calls me a cunt I am being completely reasonable.

I could have stopped this in-joke of course. Instead of cock I could call him something else. Dick and prick are out of course – having the same meaning as cock. But there's always arse or shit or pillock or bastard or plain old idiot and a million more in between. If I had chosen gender neutral language he may have done the same back. But I rather like his use of the word cunt.

Here's why. I don't deny that to many people cunt has become the most shocking swear word that can be used. But why should women's bits be so sacred that their name can't be uttered? Sure it's not very nice to call anyone after genitalia, but if we can bandy about cock and prick and dick so easily, why then gasp with horror at the word cunt?

I have a great piece of artwork on my wall by the artist Ian Stevenson. It makes me laugh every time I see it. In simple black lettering on a white background, it just says 'I cunt spell'. When I was single I worried that any man coming back to my flat might be put off by this print, but then decided I didn't want to be with anyone who might be that prudish. For by holding cunt up as the worst possible word we perpetuate this idea of women's genitalia being sacred and untouchable, even by language. This doesn't help the feminist cause a bit. Our cunts, so to speak, are equal to men's cocks in every way, which is why I think it's funny when my husband calls me a cunt.

Ovarian men

In series four of *The Apprentice*, the television show in which a group of men and women compete in business tasks to win a job with millionaire Alan Sugar, one of the competitors, Helene Speight, kept talking up her business abilities using the term 'I'm a ballsy woman.' What she seemed to mean was that she had typically male characteristics, that is, she quite literally acted like she had balls, taking risks, being curt and making tough decisions.

It's not just in the workplace that masculine language is used to illustrate how someone is acting of course. When we want to suggest that it is the woman who makes the decisions in the home we talk about women 'wearing the trousers'.

But the trouble is, none of these attributes should be considered male. Women make decisions all the time, take risks and are prepared to do tough jobs. It is pretty anti-feminist to suggest that the only way women can do these things is by becoming, if only temporarily, a man, wearing trousers or acquiring balls. But I might be happier with the language if you ever caught men talking about their communication or listening skills by adopting the same technique and boasting that they are an 'ovarian man'.

Milfs and dilfs and Wham Bam Grans

Milf has, in recent years, perhaps thanks to its use in the film *American Pie*, become part of our language. It stands of course for 'mum I'd like to fuck' and is used by men to refer either to their mum's friends or to older women who they find attractive. It's sexist on two counts of course, categorising women by their fuckability and seeing them only in terms of being a mum, not their own person. Originally milf was meant to be a little shocking – mums are supposed to be cuddly and homely and comforting, not sexy or sexual – but many women have embraced this term, though they prefer the rather more sickly sweet 'yummy mummy', and aspire to being sexual objects.

There's nothing wrong with this necessarily – why should women give up looking or feeling attractive once they have children or reach a certain age? In fact in one sense feminism has allowed this to happen – in the past women had to practically disappear from view after marriage and motherhood, giving up work and keeping house, whereas it is feminism that has led to the visibility of mothers now. But what I want to know is if we are going to label women in this way, why aren't we doing the same to men, labelling fathers who are still attractive as dilfs.

Actually, I'll tell you why. We don't have dilfs because having a word for something suggests it is unusual. Milf is slightly shocking and works as a word because we don't expect mums to be people men want to sleep with. Older men on the other hand both expect, and are expected by society, to remain sexual beings. It's the same phenomenon in which actors such as George Clooney are seen as incredibly sexy but older women actors are seen as past it. We don't have the word dilf because society sees nothing remarkable in women wanting to fuck an older man.

Older women who look for young men to sleep with have a name too. They are referred to as 'cougars'. That is, they are the hunters and the men are their prey, sucked unwillingly into their trap. The idea that a younger man would choose to sleep with an older woman for no reason other than they are attracted to her isn't one that has found itself a word yet.

Is it that shocking to suggest that older people might be fanciable? A friend suggested 'grannylicious' as the next step up from milf, women of our grandparent's generation that men are attracted to. This panders somewhat however to the idea of sweet little old ladies with hair in buns. No, I prefer Wham Bam Grans, with the suggestion of physical strength, the ability to obliterate enemies and pack a punch. I don't much care for becoming a milf as the word is so powerless – she's someone men would like to fuck rather than someone who wants to fuck men. She's sexualised but not necessarily sexual. But when I'm beyond that I wouldn't mind being a Wham Bam Gran.

3

Sex

Sex is a key part of our everyday lives, even at times when we aren't sexually active. Sex is used to sell us numerous products or forms of entertainment, even where sex itself isn't being sold. Not only that, but we are constantly judged on areas concerning sex. We are judged, not least by ourselves, on who we have sex with, on who we don't have sex with, on how often we have sex, on whether we look like we enjoy it or whether we look like we don't, and on whether other people want to have sex with us. In some parts of our society having sexual feelings, let alone sex, is seen as something to be ashamed of. In other areas it is seen as something to flaunt. Women in nightclubs are encouraged to look as sexual as possible, and then derided if men think they want it too much

Many women judge their own self-worth by whether or not

they feel they are sexually attractive to men, even if they have a partner, even if they have a successful job, even if they are, wait for it, happy. I admit to a certain buoyancy myself when someone has just tried to chat me up, even though I know this should not be how I judge myself. Take this example from the journalist Yasmin Alibhai-Brown writing in the *Independent*:

> *Last week I was at the Kitab book festival in Delhi in India. At a party for fashion week I was with two women writers and one highly respected female commissioning editor. We were in beautiful diaphanous frocks and having a great time. A British magazine male editor, fifty-two, in between cavorting with teen models, expressed his pity for women over the age of thirty because they were no longer desirable. We roared with laughter, and assured him we all had adoring lovers.*

This sounds like a wonderful evening. A party, sparkle, fabulous company. But what if Alibhai-Brown and her friends did not have adoring lovers? Would they be worth any less? Would the male magazine editor she mentions be right to feel sorry for them? Yes of course having an adoring lover is rather good fun. It is nice to be satisfied sexually. But if yes, if it is the adoring lovers who prevent these women from feeling unhappy, and if without them they would drift into a pit of despair, I do then feel rather sorry for them. Because sex is important to many of us in many different ways, but it is not so important that without it we are worthless.

I like sex!

The thing is, if you believe stories in newspapers and magazines there are two types of woman. There are those women who love sex so much they are practically tripping over their knickers in order grab the next man and slot themselves onto his cock, and there are those women who are so stingy with their sexual favours that they only give them to men in return for a nice present like some lingerie, dinner or diamonds.

They forget of course that there is a category of people, most people in fact, who actually quite like sex, and that it is possible to do so without being a sex fiend, without corrupting innocents or spreading disease or being a prostitute, without making up for a lack of self worth and without trying to get a council flat or claim benefits.

I am one of those people. That is not to say of course that I don't like diamonds or that I haven't on occasion tripped over my knickers.

Me and my 'bab

There are some things in life that when they happen to you seem absolutely normal. It's only years later, when retelling the story to someone you've just met, that you realise winning a competition to travel round the world on the basis that you're going to write a travelogue for a national newspaper on the sex and kebabs available in each country isn't that normal at all.

I blame it on the break-up. The competition, called Netjetters, had been advertised in the *Guardian* while I was still going out with the boyfriend I had met when a postgraduate student. The prize was a four month trip around the world and a weekly column on the website and in the paper. I decided I would probably apply.

Then we split up and I decided I would definitely apply. Having been an undergraduate in Manchester, arguably the British kebab capital (though most student towns will claim this title), this seemed to me an obvious way to make my entry stand out from the crowd:

> *There's a book I want to write. I've researched it extensively in England. It's called* Me and my 'bab. *It is a travel book where the history and culture of each country is examined through the consumption of kebabs. Falafel in Israel, Souvlaki in Greece and so on. I see it as a public service. I eat the kebab, I assess the kebab and the public is saved from wasting their money and toilet paper on bad examples of the kebab.*

I was twenty-three. Obviously kebabs weren't my only interest. Newly single and wondering whether I'd ever get another boyfriend, there was something else on my mind. I added another paragraph to my entry.

> *I was talking to a friend about the idea of* Me and my 'bab. *He suggested another travel book where someone must travel and have sex in every place they stop. It's an interesting idea and one I think I'd enjoy. It would certainly be a good opening line for meeting locals. I'm thinking perhaps* Me and my post-coital 'bab *would be a good way of combining the two.*

I got offered a job in China and the chance to eat and shag my way around the world in the same week. I chose what is I suppose a feminist's dream – food, sex and freedom on the open road.

When people talk to me about that trip now I try to be enigmatic. Did I really have sex and a kebab in each place they ask, and I smile in what I hope is a mysterious way. 'One or the other' I answer.

Actually, I was all mouth and no trousers. Or all mouth and all trousers, as most of the time they stayed firmly buttoned up. This wasn't a moral issue so much as a practical one. My prize included business class travel and a night in a posh hotel in each new city, after which I would be on a tight budget for the rest of my stay. So each time I arrived somewhere new I went to sleep off the jetlag in my five star bed and then the next morning transferred to a dormitory in a youth hostel. I might be sharing many of my experiences with the readers of a national newspaper, but I most definitely wasn't going to be sharing them with the other occupants of my dorm.

In one destination I did try my best to live up to my promise to readers. Arriving at my posh hotel in Toronto, I showered, put on some nice clothes and made my way down to the martini bar with a book. After a short while the waitress brought me over a drink, sent by a man on the other side of the bar. Unfortunately it wasn't the man I had been making eyes at.

I accepted the drink and the man who sent it came over to join me. I'd always wanted to be the kind of woman who could sit in a bar and men would send drinks over to. If only I was a smoker and had a long cigarette holder, I'd be the epitome of glamour I thought. It was like my favourite film, *Pretty Woman*, in which a beautiful prostitute spends a week in a posh hotel with a rich businessman and falls in love. Not that I was being a hooker, oh no.

The man turned out to be, as they say, good from far but far from good. After a short while I made my excuses and left, but buoyed by my success and fuelled by the martinis, as I walked past the man I had made eyes at originally I smiled and said 'Meet me in the lobby in five minutes.'

He did. That's when the reality hit me. I was twenty-three. Everyone who cared about me was on the other side of the world. If the man I had picked up decided to murder me, who would know? And who would I have to blame but myself? After all, the martini bars of posh hotels are exactly where murderers come to find their victims, everyone knows that. I made my excuses and fled again, this time to the safety of my room.

In fact in my four month trip I managed to have many kebabs and just one evening of sex. I toyed with not writing about it, but I felt I owed it to my readers. I would, I decided, shroud the event in mystery, give it an air of 'did I or didn't I' and hope readers would be wowed by my descriptive language instead of focusing on the physical side:

> *So you wake up and it's glorious sunshine and you walk across*
> *the Golden Gate bridge and the skyline of San Francisco glitters*

in one direction and the bright orange cables of the bridge stretch out in front of you and the bay spreads out beneath you. Even dropping your sunglasses over the edge and into the water cannot detract from the fact that this really is the most beautiful of cities.

… The man sitting next to me at the bar was reading a book of short stories by Sam Shepherd, and he said things like 'George Bush is so stupid' and he had a sense of humour and, goddammit, he was mighty fine-looking too. And we talked about literature and San Francisco and it turned out he lived in The Haight which was on my list of areas to check out. And the barman overheard and said: 'You could wake up at his house and see The Haight in the morning' and, well, it would have been rude not to after that. So we established that he was joking about the tattoo of an American eagle bearing a machine gun on his back and headed to some bars in The Haight, and though I only meant to stay for one it was obvious after a few pints that the barman had been right.

His apartment was up one of San Francisco's many hills and the back porch overlooked the Golden Gate bridge, or so he said, but it was foggy so I had to take his word for it and the next morning I rose before the fog so I never found out.

The day that week's column was published the *Guardian* gave it a plug on the front page of the website. As my dad turned on his computer to check his only daughter's progress as she backpacked around the world, he was greeted with a blue banner linking through to my article and just three words: 'Ellie has sex!'

There's not a lot I would like to apologise to my parents for. I certainly don't regret my rather wonderful night in San Francisco, or most of the rather less wonderful nights I had elsewhere in the ten years from my late teens to my late twenties. But even as a noughtie girl happy with the idea of random encounters with strangers do I think a father should ever have to read about his daughter's sex life over breakfast? However liberal my parents are, however much they have encouraged my feminism and desire to do what I want and make my own choices, and however rebellious their daughter is, I think the answer is probably no.

Teenage kicks

However having said that I don't think my sex life is something my dad should have to read about over his breakfast, I do think fathers (and mothers) need to be relaxed about their daughters' sexuality. After all, they are pleased when we learn to ride our bikes, when we learn to read, when we pass exams. They should be pleased too by every step we take towards adulthood. It makes me cringe when I hear dads joke about locking up their daughters, and about how it isn't their daughters they don't trust but the men that they might meet. Their daughter after all hopefully came out of pleasurable moments with her mother. No, daughters having sex is not something to be ashamed of but rather something parents need to come to terms with.

Nevertheless every so often there is a furore in the press about magazines for teenage girls and the sexual content. This isn't new. When I was in my early teens we went to stay with friends for the weekend and I offered the daughter, who was the same age as me, the chance to read one of my magazines. She refused, primly telling me that her mummy didn't allow her to read that kind of thing.

I don't know what her mummy thought she was going to do after reading these magazines. Was reading an article on top ten tips for snogging going to make her sneak out of the house, strip down to her underwear and walk around the streets begging for sex? It would have been quite amazing if so as the most it ever did for me was to leave my mouth tasting of pillows after practicing said snogging techniques on my bedding.

In fact teenage magazines do a pretty good job of teaching safe sex. I don't remember ever reading a magazine aimed at early teens that didn't remind girls not to do anything until they were ready, and nowadays teenage magazines all go by guidelines administered by the Teenage Magazine Arbitrational Panel that include the following stipulations:

Readers will always be encouraged to take a responsible attitude to sex and contraception, and where relevant to seek advice from General Practitioners and other professionals.

If sex is being discussed, then safer sex will be highlighted and encouraged wherever relevant.

Where under-age sex or sexual abuse is discussed it will be

*clearly stated as illegal. Under-age sex will be discouraged and
the age of consent clearly stated.*

So why is it that some people don't want teenagers to know about
sex? Is there perhaps an element of jealousy in seeing young
people discover this new area for the first time and a kind of
collective jealousy that we are no longer young, and can no longer
know teenage fumblings and the joy of those first experiences?

Certainly teenagers having sex is nothing new. Think of
Romeo and Juliet (written in the late 1500s) and thirteen year old
Juliet's explicit yearning to have sex with Romeo. In many
cultures of course getting married and having children as
teenagers is the norm. I am not suggesting we go back to this,
unless individuals want to of course – but let's not pretend
wanting sex at a young age is a new phenomenon or a
strange one.

In lots of the writing about teenagers and sex there is an
assumption that if teenagers, particularly girls, are having sex it is
because they are being pressured into it, either by boys or by
society's expectation. I am sure this is true in many cases, but
also in many cases teenagers are having sex because they want to.
This seems to be a hard fact for many people to get their head
around.

There is of course a huge double standard here. Teenage boys
are expected to have their heads full of sexual thoughts and to
find it hard to concentrate on anything else in life. It is girls who
are expected to be chaste at this age.

Of course none of this is to say that teenagers, or anyone, should have sex if they don't want to. They need to be able to explore their sexuality without actually having to have sex or feeling that it is expected of them – having the age of consent is a good excuse in this respect for teenagers who do not feel ready to have full sex – and enjoying the intensity of teenage crushes and the beginning of sexual exploration without having the expectation of having sex is important. This is important as a culture of turning a blind eye to teenage sex does mean that girls not ready to have sex are left vulnerable to coercion and because there is a danger that we normalise teenage sex to the point where girls think that is what they should be doing, rather than something they can do if they want.

But I remember being desperate to lose my virginity, even before I reached the age of consent, and this was not, I am sure, because of pressure from external sources be it boys, magazines or popular culture generally, but because as my body matured sexual feelings and a keenness to explore them were very natural.

Sluts

The zipless fuck was a term coined by Erica Jong in her novel *Fear of Flying*, published in 1973, in which the lead character, Zelda, looks for sex with a stranger she need never see again with nobody else knowing what took place. For many Western women such encounters are so commonplace nowadays it is hard to imagine what shock the concept might have held for people. In fact the rise of binge drinking goes beyond the zipless fuck – not only need other people not know you had your anonymous fuck, you might not necessarily know it yourself.

I have written a number of articles on contraception, specifically emergency contraception or the morning after pill. My articles and campaigns have lobbied for easier access to emergency contraception, making it available on the supermarket shelves, or at least over the counter in pharmacies. In attempting to counter the opposing arguments, including the one that says better emergency contraception will lead to more promiscuity, I found a study published in *JAMA*, a well respected American health journal. They found that where women did have better access to emergency contraception there was no evidence at all that they became more promiscuous. When I started writing about the subject, I included this piece of information. Then one of my contacts, a specialist in reproductive medicine, said to me 'so what if it does?' She was right of course – so intent was I on winning the argument in my article, I had lost sight of the fact that promiscuity, when safe and consenting, is not a bad thing.

Take this story about a woman I know who has been particularly promiscuous, sleeping with over a hundred men, some as part of a relationship, some as part of a torrid fling, some as a one night stand. When she fell in love with one of them, and he with her, she told him about her sexual past. His response? How lucky he was, he said, that she should choose him over all those other men she could have had.

Most men are not as enlightened as this man however. Female promiscuity is seen almost universally as a bad trait (in men of course it's 'sowing wild oats'), not just in obviously offensive words such as slag and slut but also in words that seem less judgemental at first – vamp or vixen, both of which are predatory words.

In fact, in her book *He's a Stud, She's a Slut and 49 Other Double Standards Every Woman Should Know* by the American feminist writer Jessica Valenti, the first suggestion Valenti makes on how to rectify these contradictions is: 'First and foremost, stop calling other women sluts.'

We nevertheless remain fascinated with women who openly enjoy sex, particularly if they have done so with many partners. At a dinner with friends recently I found myself telling them about my trip round the world with the mission to have a shag and a kebab in each place (see page 39). They asked whether I now regretted any of this. And I recalled a former women's magazine editor I know who took me out for dinner in my mid twenties and quizzed me about my love life. 'Nobody gets to their deathbed and wishes they had slept with fewer men,' she counselled me. (This is presuming they are not on their deathbed because of a sexually transmitted disease I guess.) But why would anyone regret their sexual experiences? Surely they make us who we are today, even the 'mistakes'.

There should not be a feminist position on how many people is the right number of people to have slept with. Whether we have slept with one person, a thousand people or with no one, shouldn't have any bearing on how we are seen by others, or even by ourselves. The only non-feminist thing about sex is judging people for it.

When mistakes happen

The current system in the UK means that it is very hard for women to obtain emergency contraception in advance to keep 'just in case', and also, depending on the time and where you are, it's not that easy to get hold of when the need does arise.

Healthcare providers prefer us to use the term emergency contraception to morning after pill because it can work in preventing pregnancy for up to seventy-two hours after having unprotected sex. However success rates of emergency contraception are much higher the sooner after sex it is taken – ninety-five per cent effective if taken within twenty-four hours of unprotected sex but only fifty-eight per cent if taken seventy-two hours later – 'morning after pill' is not too much of a misnomer.

Because the sooner after sex emergency contraception is taken the more effective it is, it would make sense for every sexually active woman or man who does not want a baby to have a supply at home, in their bedside drawer or bathroom cabinet so, in the case of an accident with other forms of contraception, it is there to be taken immediately.

However current guidelines are that emergency contraception should usually only be given out at the point of needing it. This means that if you were to go on holiday to a country where emergency contraception is difficult to get hold of, or even illegal, and had a contraceptive accident, you wouldn't be able to just go into your first aid kit and use some emergency contraception. Instead, if conception did occur, you would face the issue of whether to have an unplanned baby or an abortion.

Nor can anyone other than the woman needing emergency contraception buy it. I tried to buy emergency contraception for a friend once. She couldn't get to a pharmacist and was aware of the need to take it as soon as possible. In the first two pharmacists I visited, I told the truth – that I was buying on behalf of someone else. They refused to give it to me. In the third I lied. The emergency contraception was for me, I said. A condom had split the night before, I said. I was midway through my cycle, I said. These were all textbook answers, albeit lies, and I was given the medication and went on my way.

I had to lie because the Royal Pharmaceutical Society's (RPS) guidelines say that other than in exceptional circumstances, pharmacists can only provide emergency contraception for the person who needs it. This is left to the pharmacists' discretion, but being stuck at work or at school or at home looking after children does not tend to be deemed exceptional circumstances. This rule means mums cannot get it for their daughters nor men for their partners. And friends cannot come to the rescue.

Many people, including some pharmacists, argue that restrictions to access are there because they need to ask certain questions of women before they can take it. This suggests that women are incapable of self-diagnosing and reading instructions, and ignores the fact that we habitually self-diagnose and self-medicate for other reasons. I believe that if we are clever enough to decide when to take a headache tablet, then we are clever enough to read the instructions and decide whether or not we should take the morning after pill.

Several women I know rounded on me when I started writing about this campaign. I was overestimating the intelligence of most women they said, who have sex whenever they want (so what!) with whoever they want (so what!) and with a careless attitude to contraception. They refused to acknowledge that actually taking the morning after pill shows a responsible attitude, taking responsibility to rectify the error of unprotected sex sooner rather than later. One of the women I talked to about these proposals spoke with fear about her vision of a future in which emergency contraception is available in vending machines in pub toilets. This is not quite what I am advocating, as condoms are cheaper, more reliable and not hormonal, and are already available in pub toilets, but it was not far off what I was suggesting, which is emergency contraception available on the supermarket shelves, or failing that over the counter and on demand at pharmacies.

Contraception for men
Of course if women have to mess up their bodies with contraception, why shouldn't men? Actually neither sex has to as there are many barrier methods of contraception available that stop sperm ever getting anywhere near to the egg. But many

people don't like condoms and anyway, this book isn't a guide to what contraception you should use.

The invention of cheap, easily accessible contraception, in particular the pill but other methods also, was a huge leap for womankind. The contraceptive pill was introduced in 1961 although it was at first available only to married women, a statist attempt to stop sex outside of marriage. This changed in 1967, becoming available to all women. Once women could control their own fertility they stopped being baby making machines and became people who could compete on equal terms in the workplace, thus earning their own money and taking more control of their lives. Until then the best form of contraception was abstinence, a state that is unrealistic for most people and that prevents us exploring and enjoying our perfectly natural sexual urges. The pill also ensured that women not only had access to contraception, but that they didn't need to consult anyone (other than doctors) to take it, so we could not be made pregnant against our will.

But feminism is about equality and if women can control their reproductive systems shouldn't men be able to as well? The arguments against developing a male pill are threefold.

First is the issue of trust. Would you really trust a man to remember to take his pill every day, especially when the physical repercussions of not doing so for him are so much less than they are for a woman? As one woman I spoke to said: 'How could you trust any man to take a pill every day when they can't even be trusted to flush the loo each time they use it?' She would only be happy with a male pill that had a physical manifestation to show it had been used properly – a fluorescent penis was her possibly tongue-in-cheek suggestion.

Second however is an argument far more serious than that. If men had the option of controlling their own fertility in that way, would women ever get the babies they want? What if men never stopped taking their pill, turning off their fertility until it was too late for their partners to conceive? Is it possible that men could collectively decide to do this so that they force the situation of women having to go out with much older men in order to get the babies they want?

Some writers on this subject have suggested that the problem with a male pill is that it would end the usual way of women getting pregnant, which is that women decide when to have babies, either tricking men into it or exerting pressure on them until they give in to their partner's demands for a baby, and that without this there would never be any babies. While in many (or most, one hopes) cases babies are the result of discussion and agreement between a couple, we know this isn't always the case, and while I am not suggesting men should be tricked into having children, often it is inertia rather than active desire to have children that leads to babies – that is, the woman wants babies and stops taking the pill or using other forms of contraception and the man knows this and while not necessarily as committed to reproduction as the woman does nothing to actually stop it. I view this as a good thing because if women worked to men's timetables then we would be post menopausal by the time the thought crossed most of their minds.

Third, control over our fertility has been one of the key developments in helping women gain something nearing equality. We now choose when we have children in order to fit in with our careers or other life plans. Given that women do most of the childcare and of course carry the child, it is imperative that women have the biggest say in when this happens rather than men because much as feminists want men to realise the consequences of having a baby are as important for them as for women, this is not currently the case.

But though I have no wish to see a male pill developed, I do struggle with men who refuse to take their share of responsibility for contraception. Recently I had a conversation with a man in his thirties who said to me that he felt vulnerable because women his age want babies and he is worried they will trick him into it. 'Well just wear a condom,' I said.

Him: Yeah but it's disgusting that they might trick you into it
Me: Maybe they want babies
Him: Maybe I don't
Me: Then wear a condom
Him: What if I get tricked into it?
Me: If you're worried about them using pins then wear your own condom
Him: If you were single and wanted a baby would you do that?

Me: Well I wouldn't lie and say I was on the pill but I might
not say anything if I wasn't using contraception
Him: That's exactly what I mean
Me: Then wear a condom.

We went round and round in circles. The fact is that this man thought not having a baby was a woman's responsibility. He didn't seem to accept that if he doesn't want to get a woman pregnant then there is already a very easy way to stop it happening.

I don't dispute that there are some women who want babies who will sleep with men without contraception, hoping they get pregnant and not minding who the father is. I don't even dispute that there are some women who lie about their method of contraception. But condoms are there to empower men as well as women. They are in fact already the equivalent of a male pill and what's more, they don't mess up your body, give you mood swings or require remembering something every morning – you'd think they'd be bloody grateful.

Sex with someone you love

At school I remember one friend gossiping to me about another girl who went to a different school but who we both knew. She had, said my friend, admitted to some other girls she knew that at night she fingered herself. How disgusting, my friend said, and I agreed. I didn't want her to know that I found the idea thrilling.

Later at university, I remember a girlie chat one night in a bar. We knew all there was to know about each other in terms of heterosexual experiences from numerous games of 'I have never' and 'truth or dare', where you either admit things, usually sexual, or face dares, but we had never spoken about masturbation. Then one girl said yes, she masturbated every night, and what is more, she had done since she was about twelve. Slowly everyone said something similar.

But female masturbation, or as I like to think of it, sex with someone you love, is one of the last taboos. While we accept that men may pleasure themselves frequently, expect it even, women doing so is barely mentioned other than as a fallback for when men are not up to the job and, after rolling off you, may give you permission to finish yourself off, or as part of a repertoire designed to turn men on.

This refusal to accept female masturbation as something that women do alone, for their own pleasure and frequently is all bound up in the refusal of society at large to believe that women can be sexual beings in their own right, rather than here just to pleasure men.

Female masturbation has had something of a PR campaign with the arrival of vibrators on the high street. Now you no longer need to go into a seedy sex shop or find a specialist mail order catalogue – you can buy your vibrator while out buying a new outfit. But many vibrators are male imaginations of what women like, or what they would like to imagine we like – effectively plastic shaped into large penises or moulded to look like an animal – rabbit, beaver or other.

So what am I suggesting – that you wave your non-willy-shaped vibrators around proudly while talking loudly in bars about how you made yourself orgasm three times last night? Of course not, unless you want to that is. But it is about time women stopped colluding in the myth that sexual pleasure is the domain of men, or only achievable for women when they are with a man.

After the main course ...

In her book *Sex Tips for Girls* Cynthia Heimel wrote:

> One does not have to sleep with, or even touch, someone who has paid for your meal. All those obligations are hereby rendered null and void, and any man who doesn't think so needs a quick jab in the kidney.

This is absolutely true of course, we don't have to sleep with anyone we don't want to sleep with ever, whatever they have bought us, though I am inclined to think that if I am going to sleep with people anyway then I would rather have dinner too.

But it would be disingenuous to pretend that we don't know that some behaviour can lead to an expectation of sex and if we are to be true feminists, that is, going about our daily business with our eyes wide open to how society often operates rather than allowing the world and all its wicked ways to wash over us, then we do have to take some responsibility for the messages we give out.

My friend Sarah, before she was married, said never mind dinner, she wouldn't even let a random man in a bar buy her a drink. This was not just because she probably wasn't going to sleep with them, but because she didn't even want to feel obligated to talk to them. Talking of course can be a lot more intimate than sex, but this isn't what she meant. Her refusal to accept a drink was because of the understanding that it really is rare to ever get something for nothing. To pretend otherwise is foolish.

Sure, if you meet someone for dinner, and if they offer to pay at the end and you let them, that is not an agreement to have sex. Nor is going to someone's house for coffee. Nor is going to someone's house for coffee and kissing them. Nor is following that kiss with some fondling. And if the fondling moves to the bedroom and becomes naked fondling, even then either party can say no, of course they can. But at some point it can be argued that both parties have given clear signals that there may be sex involved.

So what does this mean? Should we never let people buy us dinner if we don't intend to sleep with them? Sad as this might be if you have a penchant for fine dining and a bank balance that prefers fast food, this is probably true. Outside of genuine mixed sex friendships or work relationships, letting a man buy you dinner isn't saying you will definitely sleep with him either that evening or in the future, but it is suggesting that you haven't yet decided you definitely won't. Or if you have decided you won't, then why let him buy you dinner in the first place?

No laughing matter: can we joke about rape?

I was on a tube train recently coming back from the Essex end of the Central Line towards London. It was about midnight so most of the travellers were going the other way. There were just two people in my carriage, me and a man in his mid twenties. I was reading a book and he asked me about it. I was drunk, but he was drunker, although in a funny rather than aggressive way. I decided he was harmless and when he started talking to me we spoke about the book I was reading. He told me he was writing a sitcom but worked in the city. I told him I had dabbled in stand up comedy. He said he'd tell me a joke.

Here is the joke:

A man walks into a bar. He looks around and says to the barman 'I could have any woman here that I want.'
'How's that?' says the barman.
'Because I'm a rapist.'

I know you might not find this joke funny. By rights, late at night in a train carriage with no means of escape and alone except for a drunk man, I shouldn't have found it funny either. But I did. He'd broken the rape taboo, the unmentionable. All women alone with a strange man in that situation will worry if he is a rapist. But it is never mentioned. This man had tackled the subject head on and I found it hilarious. The man admitted that he knew it was an inappropriate joke but I was still laughing. We chatted some more. We both got off the train at Liverpool Street. He put his arm around my shoulders and slurred 'Am I coming home with you then?' 'Thanks for the offer,' I said, 'but no thanks.' We parted amicably and went our separate ways.

I have told many women about this incident. Some, like me, have found it funny. Most have not.

I am not for one moment saying that rape isn't a horrendous thing. But the way we often deal with horrendous things is to claim them as our own and to make jokes about it. Take the following example. A couple of days after the tsunami that killed thousands of people across Asia I went to a comedy show at a London theatre. The comedian, known for being shocking, made several jokes about the tsunami. I don't remember them all. Something about a big wave to our Asian members of the audience. Tsunami being a high scorer on the game show *Countdown* (presenter Richard Whiteley had just died). The Tsunami (Toon Army) causing havoc across Asia. There were some boos, but mainly people laughed. Certainly there was a consensus that we come to terms with tragedy through humour. No one thought the comedian didn't care about the loss of life in the tsunami.

So why is it we can use humour in one bleak situation and not another? When I was at a country house party a few years ago, I stayed at a bed and breakfast a couple of fields away. I didn't want to walk back alone and I had found myself getting rather intimate with another guest, a friend of a friend. He offered to walk me back to my bed and breakfast, an offer I was grateful for – being a city girl I imagine all country fields in the dark are full of rapists waiting to attack lone women (ironically friends from the country think the city is just like this). The walk involved going around the edge of the fields which were full of the yellow flowers of a crop called rape, used for oil. 'I'm not sure about letting a strange man walk me across the raping fields' I said. This was a joke about rape. It acknowledged I might sleep with him consensually, and it acknowledged I might not. In fact it put the issue of consent right at the forefront of the conversation. He promised not to rape me in the raping fields and we spent a rather jolly night together. In this case joking about rape made me feel more comfortable, not less.

Around the same time I went to a comedy club above a pub in London. It was where established comics tried out new material. One told a long and rambling joke that went something like this.

> *I was walking home the other day and a woman was in front of me going the same way. I knew that she'd be worried I would attack her so I crossed over the road. She also crossed over the road. So I crossed back. She crossed back. This happened a few times and eventually I said to her why do you keep crossing the road every time I do. 'I didn't want you to think that I thought you were a rapist' she said.*

So far so funny.

Then the punchline.

She was quite ugly and I was concerned that she would think that I hadn't raped her because she was ugly. I didn't want to make her feel bad about herself. So I sympathy raped her.

I laughed. It was funny. We all know the idea of a sympathy shag. Turning it around was funny. But I was the only one who laughed. The rest of the audience booed. Even the other comics who, as a rule, don't boo each other.

Laughing about rape doesn't make it funny, but it does help us to work out our thoughts and feelings about a subject the way humour does in many other cases too. But I'll tell you what really isn't funny; at least 47,000 adult women are raped every year in the UK, that thirty per cent of people say a woman is partially or totally responsible for being raped if she was drunk, that up to ninety-five per cent of rapes are never reported to the police and of rapes that are reported in the UK, just one in twenty end with a conviction, the second lowest rate in Europe. Rape isn't funny, but it's not the jokes we make about rape that are the problem. The problem is our failure as a society to deal with rapists, to ensure that women feel able to report rape and that there is a high conviction rate when they do – that is the least funny thing of all.

What do I mean by rape?
Rape is about far more than sex, though I have put this section here in the sex chapter. But more than sex, rape is usually about power, and when a woman is raped her power to say no is taken

away from her. So if I were to say 'does rape matter that much?' there would be an outcry, and rightly so. And I am not about to disparage the seriousness of rape. Rape has been used systematically both as a war crime and in everyday life as a means to subjugate women. And what's worse, we are often told rape is a woman's fault, for wearing a short skirt, for being drunk, for acting provocatively or for just being there.

Rape is always wrong. I want to write that as clearly as possible. But, and this is where I expect I will get angry letters, I think we do women an injustice when we say that rape is the worst thing that can happen to a woman. It is, after all, just a penis.

Of course there are obviously many occasions when rape is coupled with violence, and that is not just a penis, that is about fear and no longer feeling safe and about being robbed of confidence. It was the feminist writer Germaine Greer who, writing about being raped herself aged nineteen, said it was not the rape itself, the sexual violation, that scared her so much as the violence and potential for violence.

But the frames of reference around rape are so often about a woman's virtue. While maintaining that rape is a terrible thing to happen, I do think we have to move away from this idea of it as the worst thing that can happen. Being raped is a horrible thing, but by buying into it as the worst possible thing that can happen, we buy into the idea of it being about taking a woman's virtue and of that being her most important asset.

Following on from this we have to address different types of rape. It is not fashionable in feminist circles to do this as it is thought to belittle some women's experiences. But traditional feminist ideas are not necessarily helpful when looking at rape from a noughties point of view. After all, one school of feminist thought in the past said that all acts of penetration were rape, something feminists have moved on from nowadays. But if we are to get rape, particularly violent rape, taken seriously as a society, we have to be able to differentiate between the circumstances in which it happens.

Let us be clear on what rape is. Sex with someone I later decide I do not like may be embarrassing but it is not rape. Changing my mind after penetration is not rape. Giving drunken consent to someone I would never have slept with if I were sober may be icky when I think about it, but it is not rape. Is it rape if you've sucked him off willingly and he's then tried to have full sex with you but you say no and he continues anyway? Yes. But is that as bad as being violently attacked by a stranger down a dark alley and not knowing whether you will live or die? No.

Many feminists decry the attempt to separate these things. But they are different. We need as a society to look sensibly at date rape, at stranger rape and at rape inside marriage, and work out our collective view on these. We need to think what consent means and whether the onus should be on having to explicitly give consent or whether it is on explicitly saying no. We need to address whether alcohol plays a role and to understand that rape is always the fault of the rapist and never the fault of a short skirt. And we need to stop equating rape with stealing virtue and see it instead in terms of assault, because a woman's virtue should never be equated with sexual activity, consensual or not.

The naked truth

Ian Stone is an intellectual comedian who does topical, thoughtful and funny routines. I heard him once musing on pornography during a show. 'Some people complain that porn objectifies women,' he said. Pause. 'Of course it does. That's the point.'

He is right of course, it is exactly the point. Porn is not supposed to be concerned with ensuring the representation of men and women is responsible or even realistic. Porn instead appeals to the side of our brains that wants to fantasise and become aroused.

The sex industry isn't just in magazines or on film of course. It happens all over the place in lap dancing clubs, sex shows and of course brothels. But should we care if our men look at porn magazines or videos, or go to 'titty bars'?

A friend of mine worked as a topless waitress when she was a student. She argues that the men were being exploited far more than she was, because she earned great money for little effort and just thought it funny that the men actually thought she might want them when she just saw them as pathetic individuals who were giving her cash.

At the opposite end of the spectrum is another friend who got thoroughly upset when her fiancé admitted to her they had been to a strip club on his stag do. That she got upset is between the two of them, but I did wonder what she thought he and his mates were doing on their weekend in Eastern Europe. Could she really have believed they would be looking at medieval churches?

I have been a consumer of porn myself. When on holiday in Amsterdam in 2002 with a female friend, we found ourselves admitting to each other that we were both interested in going to see one of the live sex shows on offer in the red light district to see what it was all about. We were in our mid twenties and had both enjoyed a varied sex life at university and after.

The show may have been about sex but it was not sexy. In a theatre with many other tourists, a couple came on and acted out a scene to music, including some penetration and pumping. So for example there might be a cops and robbers scene in which the policewoman catches a robber and then makes him have sex with her, or a Tarzan and Jane scene in which he catches her and they have sex. The entry price covered as much as you wanted and after seven or eight vignettes performed by two different couples we got a sense of *déjà vu*. The couples merely repeated the cycle, only this time a little less hard with perhaps slightly less enthusiasm, or maybe the lack of enthusiasm was us, not them.

Talking about our experience afterwards neither of us had found it particularly sexy. But supposing we had, could we still be feminist?

There are several feminist arguments against porn. Perhaps the most convincing is the idea that porn normalises the objectification of women, an idea that then enters our collective consciousness to a point where women are seen, by themselves and by men, merely as sexual objects. Some 1970s feminists went further than this. Porn inevitably led to predatory sexual behaviour in men, they said, and Susan Brownmiller famously came up with the slogan 'pornography is the theory, rape is the practice'. Set against this were 'sex-positive feminists' who disputed this and embraced women's freedom to participate in and enjoy pornography. (If you want to read a book on the pervasive nature of porn in society then I thoroughly recommend Ariel Levy's *Female Chauvinist Pigs*. She not only looks at what it is that has given us a culture where the public, particularly women, are happy to do all kinds of sexual acts to get on TV in shows such as America's *Girls Gone Wild* but also gives the reader an excellent tour through the history of feminists' attitudes to sex.)

There are of course issues where the porn industry, in the shape of lap-dancing clubs or strip joints, plays a role in business networking, leaving many people (both women and men) excluded or uncomfortable. And there are also huge issues around the extent to which people involved in porn are exploited and whether they have real choices about what they do. But to automatically decry porn as anti-feminist is not particularly helpful. As noughtie girls know, sex, and images of sex, are not inherently bad.

4

Work

P icture this. A woman is sitting on a bench outside a shiny city building, home to an international law firm. This could be anywhere from Chicago to Kuala Lumpur, from Rio de Janeiro to London. She is wearing a suit and smart high-heeled shoes. She is reading a celebrity magazine. She finishes her sandwich, has the last sip of her smoothie, brushes back her hair with her perfectly manicured fingernails and heads back into the office block.

In your mind is this woman the secretary or a partner? Those of you who are partners reading this will probably say she is the secretary on the basis that you never have time for lunch. But that aside, what makes you think it? Is it the celebrity magazine? I know plenty of intellectual, successful women, and I include myself in this, who like to read celebrity magazines. Even those of you who pretend you don't probably get a guilty pleasure from doing so in the dentists' waiting room or if you find one left behind on the train.

Perhaps the shoes give it away. They look like Prada you think, only the partner can afford that. Again, not necessarily true – think how many women you know enjoy the thrill of a bargain and love to get their designer lookalike shoes cheaply from the high street, and think about how many people that you assume don't have much money spend what they do have on designer items.

Or what about those manicured fingernails – are they so because she has been filing her nails in between jobs like the stereotypical secretary? Or because she fitted in a fifteen minute mini manicure at the salon by the station on the way home from work yesterday?

No, the truth is this woman could be a secretary and she could be a partner. Feminism has been successful thus far in that you have no way of knowing which she is. The fact that the same is not true for men – how many male secretaries do you know? – is part of the bigger picture and despite some women making it into some senior jobs, things in the workplace are far from equal.

Why most women bosses are shits

A man I know says he hopes never to work for a woman boss again. Women bosses, he says, won't accept ideas from other members of the team, like to micro-manage, can't have a disagreement without turning it into a huge argument, are poor at giving both negative and positive feedback, take everything personally and try to be best buddies with everyone and are then disappointed and vindictive when this doesn't work. To many feminists this is an outrageous statement. To me it is an outrageous statement. Other than the fact that I am inclined to agree with him. Women bosses can be absolute terrors.

Perhaps this man's – and my own – judgement of female bosses is overly harsh. After all, we don't assume all male bosses will be terrible just because we have had a bad male boss in the past.

And of course not all women bosses are awful. There are some who are fair, hardworking and keen to give a helping hand to junior members of staff to help them achieve their best. But there are also many women bosses who show the worst characteristics you can get in the workplace and make life hell for their junior colleagues.

One friend of mine who has had bad experiences with both male and female bosses thinks the problem is that we are all, male and female, conditioned to think of women as nurturing and encouraging, as the mummy figure we go to for comfort and encouragement, so both genders react badly to being managed by a woman. When she isn't that nice after all, we have a sub-conscious reaction that 'the mummy figure is being mean'.

This might be true. After all, we think of a bad male boss as just a 'bad boss' where for a woman we always add her gender – 'a bad woman boss'.

The man who first slagged off women bosses to me thinks the main problem is what he calls control-freakery, or micromanagement. A good boss, he says, has to be able to delegate and leave people to do things, something women also find hard to do in the home he says, his excuse perhaps for not doing his fair share of the housework.

And as if that isn't one stereotype too many, here's another from him. Women, he says, see themselves as good communicators based on the fact that they like talking. But, he says, this is very different from being an effective communicator.

I have a theory that because it is harder generally for women to get to the top, those who are nice people tend to withdraw from this race before they get there. Therefore it is only the women who are ruthless enough to knock down all those around them in their bid for promotion that make it, and when they do so they often adopt an 'if I did it the hard way you should have to too' attitude. The same isn't true for men because they have more opportunities, so they don't need to be as ruthless to get to the top.

I suspect that when it is as easy for women to get to the top as it is for men, we will be able to stop referring to terrible women bosses as terrible women bosses and start just calling them terrible bosses.

Equal rights for mediocre women

One country in which companies are being forced to have women right at the top is Norway, where in early 2008 a law came into effect that required forty per cent of seats on the board of all companies listed on the Oslo Bourse (stock exchange) to be women. This may seem like an extreme measure (though we could equally ask why forty per cent rather than fifty per cent) but in the UK where there is no such rule, we have hardly any women at board level.

So is positive discrimination the way forward in making the workplace more equal? Certainly it may be a good start in terms of getting women into high positions or workplaces where traditionally there have been few women. But without cultural change, positive discrimination is meaningless. You cannot just bring women into a workplace without thinking about women friendly practices – from maternity leave and flexible working to support networks and no meetings in men-only clubs.

If employment changes aren't accompanied by cultural changes, you merely let women over the wire in order to trip them up. This has been called the glass cliff phenomenon by researchers at the University of Essex who looked at situations where women make it to the top only to be set up to fail, and asked to do the impossible.

In part this happens because women have fewer opportunities at a senior level, so they have to take whatever opportunities they are offered rather than pick and choose and wait until a good one comes along, whereas men, confident another opportunity will arise, can wait for something better.

This is a vicious circle because according to researcher Michelle Ryan, part of the team who coined the term glass cliff

'Women have told us that if they succeed, they are given another risky position. They become known as firefighters.'

So should feminists support positive discrimination in the workplace? What if there aren't enough good women to fill all the vacancies? Noughtie girls are not against excellence – we think it's important to have leaders who can inspire and achieve and that means giving the job to the best candidate, man or woman. But we also recognise that women do not currently have equal chances to get to the top, and that cultural change is essential and positive discrimination may be necessary.

In 1995 the journalist Janet Street-Porter gave a lecture at the Edinburgh Television Festival in which she attacked people in her industry as being the 'four M's' – male, middle class, middle aged and mediocre. She was referring to the media but might as well have been referring to many other industries. At the moment, without positive discrimination, we have a situation where the top jobs are held by three types of people – excellent men, excellent women and mediocre men. Clearly this is not fair. And though the preferred state is to have excellent people at the top whatever their gender, we should be aiming for equality too. As Francoise Giroud, a French feminist and politician said: 'Equal rights for the sexes will be achieved when mediocre women occupy high positions.'

The glass umbrella

We've had the glass ceiling and the glass cliff, but there is another trend which we could call the glass umbrella. However much we might like to blame discrimination, it's not just men stopping women from reaching high positions, but women themselves. The glass umbrella is the invisible barrier that women put up to prevent themselves getting senior roles by making excuses not to apply such as 'I'd never get it', 'it pays too much money for me to have a chance' and 'they need someone with more experience'. All of this might be true but a man would go for it anyway, and sometimes the man who is being overly ambitious actually gets the job. The woman of course, having ruled herself out of the race and therefore not applied for the position, can't get the job.

This happened to me some years ago when I was sounded out about whether I would like to apply for a senior political journalism job. I said no because, I thought, I am more interested in writing about lipstick shades and relationships. See, there I go again, making myself out to be particularly girly when really I am interested in politics and had already worked editing a political magazine and contributing to national newspapers and weekly magazines about the subject. Actually I didn't say no. I couldn't even get the word out. The editor asked whether I had thought about applying for the job, and I let out a sound halfway between a raspberry and a splutter in shock at the thought.

It's a relief that on reflection it wasn't a position I wanted, and had I applied I am almost completely sure I wouldn't have got the job (see, there I go again). But young women are often reluctant to think themselves good enough to apply for jobs that men go for without a second thought. And when men do get them their confidence is bolstered so that they do the same a couple of years later and make another giant leap in their career. No wonder there are more men in senior positions.

The glass umbrella isn't necessarily a bad thing. Umbrellas after all protect us. By putting up our own glass umbrella we choose not to go any further because we know that getting to the top isn't always the best thing for us. Instead we choose more leisure time, more time with our families and less stress.

This is certainly true in my case. I know that I don't want to be the kind of person who books theatre tickets and has to give them away at the last minute because of a crisis at work. I don't want to spend every evening schmoozing with work people in receptions where people are looking over your shoulder for someone more important to talk to when I could be having a quiet dinner with people I actually like. And I don't want to be constantly worried about whether I can do the job or whether people are plotting to get rid of me and take my position.

This doesn't mean I don't have ambition of course. I am very ambitious, but most of my ambitions are for my personal life – to have a family, be happy, have holidays to interesting places etc – and those that are work related don't involve sacrificing any of these.

This is not just me. One woman I know who works part time and has two children, faced a similar situation recently:

My husband and I were both offered promotions on the same day recently – his to take on the news editorship of an additional magazine, mine to take on a campaigns role on the two days a week I don't currently work. He accepted, I declined. That is no criticism of him, it was my choice not to accept because I (usually) enjoy spending two days a week with my youngest child, but it is a compromise that men rarely have to make.

So the glass umbrella isn't necessarily a bad thing, but a choice we make. The bad thing is that because it is women doing the bulk of the caring roles and domestic duties, they often realise the best thing for them is to go no further and to put up their own barriers. Men don't have to put up the glass umbrella because there are fewer domestic duties calling for their time outside of the workplace – that is, they're not going to get rained upon anyway.

Glued to the floor

We mustn't confuse the glass umbrella or glass ceiling with what the journalist Polly Toynbee calls being 'glued to the floor' – a term she uses to describe women who are stuck in menial jobs:

Ambitious women hit their head on glass ceilings, but worse is the fate of women glued to the floor: two-thirds of the low-paid are women. The jobs they do – caring, catering, cleaning, cashiering – are low paid because they always were 'women's work'. For as long as the minimum wage stays below a living wage, woman and children will stay poor. Most poverty would be solved if the jobs women do were equally valued. But the old attitudes remain: women are 'natural' carers, cooks and cleaners.

There is an obvious answer here – to raise the minimum wage to a living wage, but nevertheless women are likely to remain the main holders of these jobs. Perhaps what we need to do is start valuing these jobs more not just in monetary terms but in terms of status and importance.

On the other hand, as the sociologist Tony Chapman points out in the book he edited on the division of labour, *Ideal Homes*, it is patronising to assume that women's work is always undignified, isolating and boring. He argues in relation to the home, but the same can be said of the workplace, that workers in these 'women's jobs' often have more control over how they do their work than men in oppressive manual work and that if having control is the key to modern happiness then women in cleaning and domestic work may not be getting the bad deal that is automatically assumed.

When I was at school teaching was not seen as a great profession. The salaries were bad and the saying 'if you can, do, if you can't, teach' was often bandied about to disparage teachers and teaching. But in recent years this has changed. Better salaries and clearer career progression has returned teaching to a job with status.

We need a similar revolution for 'women's work', with caring, cooking and cleaning being seen as skilled and valued work. It has already begun with Jamie Oliver's campaign on school dinners and the way we have started, in the light of this, to view dinner ladies (a term which in itself assumes men will not do this job) and school cooks. It is our responsibility to ensure this continues, by making sure we never denigrate the kind of jobs that women tend to get, and that we work to acknowledge the importance of these jobs and the people who do them, while at the same time refusing to see these jobs as being exclusively for women.

Sweating the small stuff

At a meeting once in one of the jobs I have had, I was asked, when the secretary couldn't make it, to take the minutes. I refused. Not because I am a difficult bugger who prefers to doodle in meetings than take notes, though that too, but because I felt that as a woman in a mixed sex room, and the youngest by at least twenty years, if I did take the minutes I would be contributing to the idea of women in secretarial roles.

I've always been difficult. I had a teacher in my final year of junior school that I did not see eye to eye with at all. One day she set half the class, a mixture of boys and girls, some model making to do – a brilliantly fun activity. I was one of the lucky model makers. But the other half of the class who weren't making models were split up again, with the boys doing woodwork and the girls doing sewing. Aged ten I was furious. I walked into the teacher's classroom where she was in fact talking to some parents, and asked her why the non-model making boys were doing woodwork and the non-model making girls were doing sewing. She went mad at the interruption and I got a thorough telling off later. But I never did get a satisfactory explanation. That I was the only one to complain should have told me even then that feminism is not a populist position.

One friend of mine, who works in financial services in the city, said the best piece of advice she was ever given was to never ever serve the tea or coffee in a meeting where there aren't as many women as men present, however thirsty you may be, as pouring the hot drinks reinforces the stereotype that this is a woman's role.

And it is little things like this that, especially in the workplace, we must remember if we are to change the culture and assumptions of what women do and what men do.

When I grow up I want to be a man

It's not just how women are treated once they are in work that holds them back, but their ambitions long before they make it into the workplace.

One mistake we often make as a society is to think that women can only be like other women. For example, when I knew that I wanted to be a journalist, my grandparents, who would have been encouraging whatever I said I wanted to do, said 'Oh yes, like Eve Pollard.' Eve Pollard was a well known figure in the 1980s and early 1990s, having been editor of the newspapers the *Sunday Mirror* and *Sunday Express* and *Sunday* magazine for *News of the World* and *You* magazine for the *Mail on Sunday*.

Actually I wanted to be more like Nina Myskow, a journalist perhaps better known for being a panellist on the TV talent show *New Faces* but who I knew from being a panellist on Friday afternoon episodes of *Through the Keyhole* that I watched with my grandparents after they had collected us from school, as they did every Friday. (Had I known that her column for the *Sun* and the *News of the World* was called 'The Bitch on the Box' perhaps my feminist instincts would have made me like her less). But Eve or Nina, the point is the same – why could I only want to be like other women journalists?

Women need role models, of course they do. We can't all be pioneers, leading the way into unknown territory, being the first to take on a new role or break new ground, and often it is great to have a woman who has gone before us, to whom we can point and say I want to be like her. When another woman has done the hard work for us, that is very helpful – she has normalised the idea of a woman doing whatever it is she has done. But we need to know, and to teach our daughters, that we can be like the men who have gone before us too.

There is that often cited riddle about a father and son being taken to casualty after an accident and the doctor walking in to the room to treat the child only to exclaim 'That's my son.' How can it be his son, we are expected to think, if the child's dad was also in the accident. The answer is of course that the doctor is his mother. The riddle, if we fail to get the answer, is supposed to expose our instinctive sexism in assuming doctors are men.

I have known this riddle for many years. Yet still a recent news story about a honeymooning couple murdered in Antigua led me to make sexist assumptions of my own when I saw the BBC headline 'Doctor Dies in Honeymoon Shooting.' Poor woman, I thought, losing her husband so soon into their marriage. It didn't cross my mind that the doctor might be a woman. The tabloid press clearly realised their readers would make this assumption. Their headlines read 'Bride Killed on Honeymoon.'

So the doctor in the riddle is a woman. If she has a daughter then perhaps she will want one day to follow in her mum's footsteps. But if the doctor in the riddle were a man, it is okay for her to want to follow in his footsteps too – we should remember that.

Old girls' clubs

I hate women's networking events. The passing of business cards, the trying to be better than everyone else, the pretence that you want to help others rather than climb the greasy pole yourself. But if there's one thing I hate more than women's networks, it's men who try to dismiss the need for them.

I posted a request on a journalist forum asking for the contact details of a women's journalist network some time ago. A male member of the forum called Michael replied, not answering my question but instead attacking the idea of such networks. He wrote:

> Given that so many women now have high-profile, successful jobs in all branches of the media, I can't honestly see the point of such an organisation.

Urgh! I replied:

> *For many years men have been at the top of the profession. In fact men have been all over the profession, not just at the top. I'm sure people can name a few women who have made it but they are the exceptions. In many cases, particularly in the media, though this applies to all professions, the men have got their jobs through their networks – either school networks, college networks, drinking networks, union networks, sporting networks or organisations such as the Masons. This doesn't apply to all men of course, but it does to many.*
>
> *Such networks have been inaccessible to women for some time. In part this is because some are closed to women as a definite policy, in part because they are not the kind of places women always feel comfortable, in part because women usually have more caring and home commitments than men so don't have the time and in part because you need there to be women involved in order for other women to get involved (not everyone is the kind of person to be a pioneer) so it's a vicious circle.*

I went on to tell him that women–only networks redress the balance slightly, and are a necessary first step in introducing women as a whole into networking, making them feel comfortable and like they belong in this kind of career. Perhaps in due course our generation will be seen as the pioneers by future generations, who will look back in wonder that women only networks were necessary at all.

I failed to convince him.

Helen McCarthy authored a report on women's networks for the think tank Demos and found three reasons for their existence. First was for the psycho-social benefits, providing friendship and support and a place where you can talk about your problems and share your frustrations with other people who know where you're coming from – a kind of self-help group philosophy. Second was for concrete career benefits: they provide opportunities for professional development, access to information and the chance to hear about job opportunities and developments in the industry. And the third is to act as a pressure group and raise awareness of gender diversity issues generally, acting as a focus for discussion on those issues, and taking action and making sure women's voices are heard. Most networks, says McCarthy, are a combination of all three.

But for me the main reason for supporting women's networks isn't one of these bold feminist approaches to bringing equality to the workplace. No, I am in favour of women's networks merely to piss off people like Michael, who don't think we need them.

Defeminising ourselves

My friend Jennifer works as a government adviser. One thing she has noticed in particular is that where women do make it to the top they feel that in order not to draw attention to themselves as a woman, they almost have to reinvent themselves as a genderless person. While it's okay for male MPs, or Chief Executives or business owners to be enthusiastic about traditionally male interests like football, and it's even encouraged as proof that they are just a normal bloke, the minute a woman in the same position expresses interest in a traditionally feminine pursuit she is pounced on for being fluffy.

So women in these positions are not encouraged to speak about their love of shopping or fashion or cooking. For these are not seen as interests that suit leadership, that is, they are not male.

When I worked for a political think tank I used to enjoy going into the office with a celebrity magazine in my bag. Often there was a serious publication too, and I used to enjoy confusing people who didn't see how one person could like reading both. I remember one woman telling me that the magazine I had wasn't the kind of thing they read in that office. But I wonder what kind of person is so serious they can only enjoy the cerebral reading, or so vacuous as to only enjoy the magazine. Surely most people in all kinds of jobs enjoy both. I should have hidden my magazine between the pages of more suitable reading.

Not only does not allowing people to have their own interests, low-brow as well as high-brow, typical of their gender as well as less stereotypical pursuits, place unrealistic expectations on people, but it prevents them from being able to be themselves and show that they are well-rounded people with multiple interests, which is just the kind of person we should want in charge.

5

Play

What do feminists do in their spare time? Well much like the rest of the population, we have a variety of interests. We may like to socialise and go to pubs or restaurants, go for walks or drink coffee. Some feminists like to read, others can't bear it. Some feminists like to jog – I for one can't think of anything worse. Some feminists are fans of arts and crafts and knitting, some even like needlework. Some feminists are into caving or climbing or mountaineering. Some like fashion magazines and some prefer motor sports – some even like both. Other feminists may like baking or shopping. Some are fans of horse riding and country pursuits. Others of us like to sit around scratching our arses and watching television. I think you get it by now – feminists, and noughtie girls in particular, have many interests. Some of these may be typically female pursuits – perhaps some noughtie girls like embroidery. Others maybe be not typically associated with women. That's the point you see, noughtie girl feminists are just like anyone else with a whole host of interests and hobbies. The difference is that we have confidence in our interests not defining us in terms of whether we are feminist or not, which is why we don't feel we have to automatically disregard 'fluffy' interests and take up masculine pursuits.

What's more, we take the notion of free time to pursue our interests as a given. Our refusal to be the sole caregiver for our children, or to spend all our time polishing furniture, or to cook every single meal from scratch, or to work horrendously long hours every week, means we have time for ourselves, not just to work but to play.

The funny side of feminism

One of my interests is stand-up comedy. In the mid noughties I took a course in it. I was being asked to do bits and pieces on radio and TV and I wanted more experience in front of a micro-phone. Over three months I developed a five minute routine which we performed in a graduation show and I went on to perform in some comedy clubs around London.

I look quite sweet, or I did then. I'm plump and curly haired. I have a dimple. My voice sounds young. I would go on stage and say 'I know what you're thinking. You're looking at me and thinking cute.' At this stage I'd point at someone in the audience, 'Bubbly.' I'd point at someone else, 'Sweet.' I'd point at another, 'Bouncy.' I'd point at one more and pause. 'Takes it up the arse.' They laughed. 'Well,' I'd say, 'some of those are true.' Laughter. 'I am bouncy. By which I mean fat. Actually I do have an eating disorder. I am half bulimic.' Laughter.

And so I'd go on. The first joke of the night was about whether or not I have anal sex, the second was about my weight.

It is possible I was never cut out for a career as a stand-up comedian, although my jokes were pretty well received. But in the end it wasn't my lack of enthusiasm for performing at 2am to a crowd of pissed students that scuppered this alternative career, though that was a large factor. Nor was it the quality of my material. No, I stopped wanting to get on stage as soon as I met my partner.

When I started stand-up I was single. I could get up on stage and include jokes about sex and poke fun at myself knowing that the only person I might upset was myself. I am sure my partner wouldn't mind if I wanted to carry on doing this. But now I have made a commitment to him I would feel awful putting myself forward for judgement by others.

What is more, this has come entirely from me, not him. If I wanted to continue performing stand-up, with or without the smutty stuff, I know my husband would encourage me to try to achieve all that I wanted and be proud of me.

So why am I letting the thought of him stop me? Perhaps he gives me the attention I was looking for from stand-up, so now I don't need attention from strangers. Perhaps I was hoping a member of the audience would fall in love with me, or at the very least want to shag me, and now I don't need that either. Or perhaps I am using him as a convenient excuse because actually I don't want to be a successful comic, I want to curl up on the sofa with a duvet and a bag of crisps and watch light entertainment all evening. But however supportive he'd be, I'm not so sure about whether he'd approve of my favourite joke in my routine.

'My flatmate is really attractive', I'd say (the flatmate was imaginary). 'He's really into food and he gets a box of organic fruit and vegetables delivered every week, paying over the odds for muddy misshaped maggoty food. And I just don't get it,' I would add pointing at my crotch. 'I mean, my box is organic and he could eat that for free any time.'

Don't judge me by the cover of the book I am reading
I love reading what is commonly known as 'chick lit'. Chick lit is often characterised by pink or green or yellow book covers with gold or silver raised lettering or an embossed shoe or handbag on the front cover. I buy them cheaply in charity shops and read them in the bath before handing them to my friends. And shhh, don't tell anyone but I also buy them full price and read them in the evening, not to fill in time while travelling to work or to fill five minutes before a meeting starts, but as an activity in its own right. This book itself looks like chick lit, and I am proud of that because I know that this in itself doesn't mean that I am not making important points.

Contrary to what the chick lit snobs would like to believe, chick lit is about more than a woman finding a man. Sure, the hero of our story sometimes does find a man, but often they get rid of a useless man, or discover that things other than a man will make them happy. Chick lit can tell stories about best friends, about mothers-in-law and about colleagues. I've read chick lit about drug addiction, about career changing, about widowhood and about being a single mother.

Now I know that just because I read and enjoy chick lit, I am not intellectually vacuous, or as my husband calls it, intellectually flaccid (make of that what you will fellow feminists, him using the language of the penis to refer to a brain). I know this because not all chick lit is bad literature but also because I don't read it to get the same experience I might get reading prize winning novels or classic literature, I read it because I want the experience that chick lit gives me – an easy read, a clear story arc and characters I can identify with.

The phrase 'chick lit' is in itself derogatory. Similar novels aimed at men are rarely referred to as dick lit, though they might as well be, with their characters having sporty cars, huge record collections, football season tickets and other penis extensions. But chick lit suggests that this is reading for women only, or not just women but 'chicks', women not even bright enough to be afforded the title of women.

None of which matters of course for it is the readers and writers of chick lit who are happiest – the writers sell more copies and make more money than most highly regarded authors, and the readers find fulfilment and friendship, if only for the few hours it takes to read them. And I am never ashamed to show the cover of my chick lit, I never attempt to hide it between the covers of something more high-brow, because as a noughtie girl I am comfortable enough in my own intelligence to know that just as you shouldn't judge a book by it's cover, you shouldn't judge me by the cover of the book I am reading.

Why the lack of ladies loos is taking the piss

Going to the toilet shouldn't really be classed as 'play', but the fact is if you want any kind of life outside of the home then loos become a big issue. In fact ask any women what would improve their every day quality of life and sooner or later you will get to the issue of the public toilet.

It is not so much the need for the correct change, the lack of loo roll, the congealed soap, the syringes left by drug users, the cracked mirror or the stench that is the issue, though we would all like to see that changed, but the mere lack of public loos.

I have an intimate knowledge of the public loos of London, the city in which I live. I know that if I am in town and need the loo then the best bet is to head to the tube station at Green Park or Westminster, both of which have them. When I am on the edge of the city I know there is a cabin loo at the end of Hatton Garden which is not too unpleasant. I know that a big bookshop on Piccadilly has toilets, and that though another bookshop in Islington has one which says it needs a code from customer services to get in, the door is never locked so you can walk right in. I know the pubs with a side door leading directly to the stairs to the toilet. And I know the department stores with toilets and the quickest route from main entrance to cubicle.

Now it may be that I have a particularly weak bladder, but I need to wee a lot. I imagine this will only get worse if I have children and when I am old. Men need to wee too of course, but the current lack of loos is less difficult for them to negotiate as a quick pee behind a tree or up an alley is far easier for a man, though of course a disgusting habit. But because of biology, and despite some attempts to make peeing as easy for women as it is for men with the invention of contraptions such as the 'she-pee' funnel to help women pee standing up, this really is a women's issue.

Julie Neuberger takes up this fight in her book on old age *Not Dead Yet*, looking at the need for more public loos from the perspective of older people who risk being confined to their homes because of the risk of being 'caught short'. She quotes Rosemary Behan in *The Times* calling for a Compulsory Provision of Clean Public Toilets Act:

> *Britain is facing a desperate situation. That most necessary and appreciated of civic facilities – the public lavatory – is in danger of extinction. So many have been closed or sold off and turned into sandwich shops, florists, curry houses and even recording studios that their numbers have dwindled by forty per cent since 2001 … The provision of clean public lavatories is a basic necessity for any civilised country. The lack of them is an affront to our freedom.*

Most women know of course that there is more to women's loos than just having a wee, though it is in order to have a wee safely, and whenever I need one, that I wholeheartedly support Behan's and Neuberger's campaign.

There is something mysterious about women's toilets. I've made more than one proper friend through getting chatting in the loo, and several temporary friendships. Men often wonder what happens in the loo when we take a long time. The usual answer of course is queuing. There are hardly ever enough women's toilets. But sometimes chatting comes into it, or retouching make-up or lending someone a tampon, or checking someone who is throwing up is okay. Sometimes the loo is the only place we can go for a few minutes by ourselves before rejoining the group. Other times of course the loo is the inquisition chamber. I took a male friend to the theatre with me once in a mixed group. I said I was going to the loo and then every other woman did too, following me to the ladies in single file where they could then quiz me about the nature of our relationship. And of course loos are for crying in too, for comforting other women, friends or strangers, and commiserating with them about the cause of their upset – usually men.

I've been to some bars and restaurants where the toilets or the washing area are unisex. I had always thought this a good idea in theory but I hate it in practise. Would I ask another woman for a tampon there? Would I cry or let out a scream of frustration? No, women's loos are not just for peeing, but a whole lot more that should perhaps remain one of the secrets of our sex.

Not having enough public loos not only puts a stop to this, but is a serious impediment to the lives of many women.

The right to binge drink

There are of course some very obvious reasons why women, and men, shouldn't binge drink. The health risks are phenomenal with binge drinking a contributing factor in liver cirrhosis, cancer, strokes, pancreatitis, gastritis, high blood pressure, fertility problems, impotence and mental health disorders. It's not just health that binge drinkers are putting at risk. Both men and women who binge drink are far more likely to be the victims of violence too. Looked at sober, the risks are horrible. But why is it that women who binge drink are judged far more harshly than men?

A large part of this is that there is still an expectation on women to be ladylike. Ladylike includes being dainty, delicate and always appropriate (or rather, what men and women of older generations think of as appropriate). You can see this in the term used for the first binge drinking celebrities to be in the press – Zoë Ball, Sara Cox and Denise Van Outen – who were labelled 'ladettes' for embracing an alcohol fuelled nightlife with the same vigour as their male colleagues. Ladette of course is the opposite to lady as it is about trying to be one of the lads.

The other objection to girls binge drinking is the risk factor. If I were the mother of a teenage girl who went out drinking and ended up lying in the gutter, legs akimbo, I too would be worried about her safety. But remember, being so drunk you have passed out does not count as consent. It is not women who should be blamed for being sexually assaulted, whatever state they may be in, it is the attackers themselves. To suggest otherwise is akin to saying women shouldn't wear short skirts in order to prevent rape, something I think we're over.

No, binge drinking is horrible. It is undignified and poses health risks. But it is no worse for women than for men, and never an excuse for other people's bad behaviour.

As well as girls drinking more, they are also getting more violent, it's official. Home Office statistics from May 2008 showed a twenty-five per cent increase in crimes committed by girls aged between ten and seventeen in a three year period. This has included gang violence, assault, robbery and murders. It's horrific of course, both the age of the perpetrators and the level of violence. But as with binge drinking, should we be more horrified by female violence than we are by male?

We think of women as nurturing and maternal, as people who cuddle and kiss and make things better, not as people who inflict pain. It's not true of course – some of our most notorious murderers have been women (think Myra Hindley or Mary Bell) and some of our female rulers have been the most brutal (think Elizabeth I).

The right-wing journalist Melanie Phillips, writing in the *Daily Mail*, blames feminism in part for this:

> *As a result of the feminist revolution, women have commandeered the freedoms and entitlements of the masculine world …*

Along with this has come an aggressive and self-centred approach to the world which apes the worst caricatures of male behaviour. Whereas men were once associated with one-night stands, now women demand sex without strings and bring children into the world without a father as their 'human right'. Told to be assertive, they have interpreted that as being aggressive. Female role models in movies, video games or rap music increasingly glorify violence too.

The problem with feminism, she adds, is that modern feminism has reinterpreted equal rights as equal wrongs, with men and women having to lead identical lives even if this includes violent or irresponsible behaviour we would more normally associate with men. 'The outcome,' says Phillips, 'has been serious confusion among girls about their role in the world and how they should behave.'

Previous generations of feminists, she says, would be horrified by the behaviour of today's girls:

For their feminism was based on the belief that women were different from men – and worthier than them. Indeed, they wanted women to play an equal role in the public sphere precisely because they believed that women's superior moral virtues – sobriety, chastity, self-discipline – would civilise public life.

My colleague at the university where I teach, the feminist journalist Angela Phillips (no relation to Melanie) takes a similar tone in an article on binge drinking for the *Guardian*, criticising other journalists for being pre-occupied with what she ironically calls 'a woman's right to get uproariously drunk'. Like Melanie Phillips, she thinks women are better than that: 'There's a useful slogan I remember from the early days of women's liberation: "I don't want equality with men – I was hoping for something better." '

Of course I agree with both Angela Phillips and Melanie Phillips that public drunkenness is horrible and that violence is unacceptable, and that is true whether the perpetrators are male or female. But harking back to traditionally feminine values such as sobriety and chastity as Melanie Phillips does, and claiming that women are better than men, as both women do, does not help the feminist cause for equality a jot. As Victoria Dutchman-Smith writing on this subject for the feminist website *The F Word* wrote regarding this view:

> *Now, call me a crazy radical, but I believe that feminism, amongst other things, was about the right of women to behave as wickedly (or as virtuously) as men. It's what we call equality, and it's non-negotiable. The rewarding of equal rights is not conditional upon such rights being used responsibly. All-round benefit is not the standard, nor should it be. Equality is an absolute good in its own right.*

Dutchman-Smith is absolutely right. I don't want to be superior to men in my behaviour. I just want there to be a level of behaviour in society that is acceptable, and that level to be the same for men and for women.

After a night at play

Getting home is, of course, a key element in a good night out. What fun is a night with friends if you worry about your trip home in the dark? A great start has been made in London with the licensing of mini-cabs so that customers know what stickers to look for on the windscreen to know they are legitimate cabs, rather than chancers waiting to pick up drunk women. But far more could of course be done, not only to make women feel safe, but men too.

So what else do we need? We need conductors on buses and guards on trains, so that there is always a member of staff within shouting distance in case of attack, and all stations to be staffed. We need safe conditions for night workers and far better street lighting. We need flat shoes so that we can run if in danger. We need higher conviction rates for people who do attack us both as a deterrent and to keep dangerous people off the streets. And we need an awareness of the specific fears and issues that women have.

For example, I was once asked to fill in for someone running some training sessions on a notoriously rough estate in South London. The first week was fine – there were staff around and a full class. The next week, I trudged there in pouring rain to find that most people had decided to stay at home. There was just one student, a man, and no other members of staff around. I have no reason to think that this man was anything other than a normal decent man with no intention of attacking me, but alone with an unknown man in an unknown area without the security of any staff, I felt decidedly uncomfortable, and cut the class short to go home.

In Jessica Valenti's *Full Frontal Feminism* she also addresses this fear factor:

> *When I was in college, a teacher once said that all women live by a 'rape schedule.' I was baffled by the term, but as she went on to explain, I got really freaked out. Because I realised that I knew exactly what she was talking about. And you do too. Because of their constant fear of rape (conscious or not), women do things throughout the day to protect themselves. Whether it's carrying our keys in our hands as we walk home, locking our car doors as soon as we get in, or not walking down certain streets, we take precautions ... And we're so used to feeling unsafe that we don't even see that there's something seriously fucked up about it.*

If we don't address this fear, whether it is real fear borne out by statistics or imagined fear based on scare stories and media exaggeration, we make women prisoners of their own fear. And there is no point having the freedom to go out when we want, to drink as much as we want, to meet who we want and to do what we want with them once we've met them, if we're too scared to get home afterwards.

Anyone here read magazines, been raped and speak English?

I love magazines and always have, from days spent designing my own as a child and thinking about what my pocket money would buy as prizes for readers' draws (I always decided on a new pencil case I seem to remember) to my excitement at seeing new issues on the shelf.

I love the real life stories and the advice columns, the pictures of upcoming trends and lists of what's hot and what's not. I love feeling part of a community of readers. It's why I became a journalist, because I love magazines.

Nevertheless, I understand that beneath the promises to give us more confidence, better fashion sense and extra skills in the bedroom, they are not always that great for women. As one of my friends puts it, they can create want where there was no want, worry where there was no worry and insecurity and feelings of inadequacy where before there were none.

In particular, many magazines want on their pages what Jennifer Baumgardner and Amy Richards in their book *Manifesta* call the 'über victim', the woman who has faced huge challenges and against the odds survived.

Unlike in serious newspaper journalism, where one editor is known for asking young journalists for the five most important attributes in journalism and only giving them the job if they answer 'accuracy, accuracy, accuracy, accuracy and accuracy', in the world of glossy magazine journalism, accuracy is not always the highest priority. Editorial teams often come up with ideas before they have found any case studies to back them up. It's not unusual for an editor to call a freelance journalist and say something like 'We're doing a piece on battered women who found inner peace by setting up a yoga retreat' without first knowing whether there are any. The journalist is then expected to find women who fit the bill, finding someone who was beaten up enough and is now successful enough. The journalist may think this is not too hard at first – there are lots of support groups for battered women after all and many yoga retreats, surely there must be a crossover somewhere. Yet once you find an example you must submit a picture of your case study to your editor to decide whether she is pretty enough and thin enough to feature in the magazine.

This crassness isn't just a feature of women's magazines. The war reporter Edward Behr wrote a book about covering foreign conflict called *Anyone Here Been Raped and Speak English?*, a question asked of survivors after a siege at Stanleyville in Eastern Congo in 1964. But had this been for a women's magazine, he may well have said 'Anyone here pretty and a size ten who has been raped and speaks English?'

The result of this is that not only do readers start to think that all successful women have triumphed over adversity, but that they all look particularly nice while doing it. These women are then used to warn us about what could happen if we are not careful – our partner could leave us, we could go broke, we could get breast cancer.

All of this may make a great read. As I have said, I love women's magazines. But they don't necessarily make us feel good about ourselves.

A group of students at the university where I teach had to create a magazine from concept to finished product. All women in their early twenties, they decided to reject the idea of glossy magazines as we know it and instead create an intelligent arts magazine aimed solely at women and featuring women artists. 'We operate on the assumption that not all women want to know how to seduce their man with the perfect shade of lippie or what their preferred sexual position really says about them' said one of the students. They created an arts magazine called *Siren*.

She was however careful not to tie herself in too closely with the word feminist:

> *I see* Siren *as a feminist magazine in so far as it's a magazine that does not patronise women but we're not a feminist magazine in the same vein as Spare Rib. I think those magazines absolutely have a place ... but magazines should be enjoyable and engaging as well as challenging. After a long day at the office, sometimes an impassioned diatribe on how men are screwing us over in the workplace is the last thing we feel like reading.*

This shows perhaps the essence of the modern feminist, or noughtie girl – she does not want to be earnest all the time or feel the need to be political in all that she does. And although not labelled as particularly feminist, the magazine showed a confidence in feminism that takes it as a given rather than a fight to be fought every minute: 'The fact that we are a publication which caters for and features intelligent women makes us by default, a feminist publication, but we don't feel a need to assert our "girl power" on every other page' said one of the team.

Whether however, if the magazine became a frequent publication, they would be able to feature ugly artists or fat ones without a second thought, without referring to their looks or airbrushing photographs of them, remained to be seen.

A sporting chance

Among the pats on the back for our haul of medals and musings about the cost of hosting the 2012 Olympics in London, an interesting story came out at the end of the 2008 Beijing Olympics. Women competitors were complaining that there are fewer medal opportunities for women – that is, fewer competitions.

In fact there are only 127 gold medals available to women compared with 165 available to men. In cycling for example there are seven events for men and just three for women. This time, competitors have complained and what's more, perhaps because the UK were winning medals, people seem to agree with them.

One of my favourite Olympic sports is pole vaulting. To watch that is – it is unlikely that I would ever actually run with a pole, let alone let go of it and throw myself over a marker. As a child watching the Olympics I remember wondering in 1984, and in 1988, and then again in 1992 and 1996, why there was no women's pole vaulting. I knew even then, aged six in 1984, that I was unlikely to be destined for sporting success, but I remember feeling the injustice of women not being able to pole vault. Women's pole vaulting was finally introduced in 2000 at the Sydney games and I enjoyed watching it just as much as the men's competition. Since then other sports for women have also been introduced – weightlifting in 2000 and wrestling in 2004. Women's football has been an Olympic sport since 1996.

It's not just in Olympic medals though where there is a sporting disparity between men and women. Women footballers at the very top of their game can rarely afford not to also have day jobs. Arsenal Ladies for example have seen huge success since they were set up in 1987, winning twenty-nine major trophies including one Women's UEFA Cup, three domestic Trebles, ten Premier League Titles, nine National League Cups and nine FA Cups. Yet a season ticket for Arsenal Ladies costs £20. In comparison a season ticket for the male team in 2006/07 cost between £885 and £1,825,or £100,000 if you wanted the four year 'diamond package'.

But the tide is turning, a little at least. 2007 was the first year that tennis champions at Wimbledon had the same prize money whether they were a man or a woman, after many years of complaints from women's groups and players, thus sending out a loud and clear message that women are equal to men.

It would be nice if women's football was as much a part of the national consciousness as men's football, and if women could win as many gold medals as men, but ensuring prize money is the same is a good start. Now we just have to get rid of the little skirts and the lycra knickers that make sportswomen look like sex objects, and we'll be away.

6

The body beautiful

Whether others consider us to be beautiful has a big effect on our lives. An article on the CNN website in 2005 said that studies showed doctors give better care to attractive patients, attractive students get more attention and better marks from teachers, attractive people earn more and even attractive criminals get lighter sentences than ugly ones. This didn't just apply to beauty, but also to height and weight with people who are short or overweight fairing less well than taller slimmer people, particularly in the workplace.

Of course definitions of beauty have changed over history. Skin tone, bottom size, hairline and lip shape all go in and out of vogue when it comes to what is considered beautiful. What's more, most of these are areas we can do nothing about, at least without expensive, painful and dangerous surgery.

Unlike previous generations of feminists, noughtie girl feminism is compatible with aspiring to external beauty should we so wish. If we want to wear make-up, if we want to wear clothes that we think others will find attractive, if we want to present ourselves in a way that we hope others will find attractive, we can do so, and we don't have to pretend this is just for our own self-esteem. But at the same time we know that judging someone by the clarity of their skin or the jiggle of their arse is not remotely feminist, and we strive not to do so.

I was beautiful once

If I ever write a musical it will include a song by a grotesque old woman, her face painted on, wearing a cocktail dress in the privacy of her own home. She will have a number all to herself. The spotlight will be on her and she will open her mouth and sing a song called *I was Beautiful Once*. It will be haunting, sad and wistful. 'I was beautiful once' she will sing. 'With only one look, men would fall for me hook, line and sinker.' She'll describe how she turned heads, would beckon a man and get him, and how they would do as she desired. Then there will be a key change, and we'll find out there was no happy ending. 'But I forgot,' she'll sing, 'to be kind, and learn to be witty. I thought I'd get by through just being pretty. I forgot to learn friendship, and having good grace, and thought I'd get friends through my sweet little face.' And then the music slows down and she laments: 'I was beautiful once you know. But once is no good you know. Now my looks have all left me and nothing is left of me but I was beautiful once you know.'

Ah, those women who are so beautiful that they don't need to try hard at anything else. They can walk into a room and the men flock to them, and women want to be their friend and become part of the glamorous set. And of course occasionally you find one who is nice with it, but too often they have never had to cultivate any other good qualities. And then one day they are no longer beautiful, and when their looks are gone they spend their time remembering 'I was beautiful once.'

Some women think they should be applauded for being born beautiful, as if it's a personal attribute they have cultivated. Not that there is anything wrong with beauty – I like looking at beautiful people as much as anyone – but looks do not a good person make.

This works the other way too. I know a beautiful woman, the kind that men and women stop in the street to stare at and white van drivers wolf whistle when they pass. People that meet her properly often expect her to be a bitch, when in actual fact she's a great person and friend. Yes, beautiful women can also be clever and nice and kind.

It's wrong to argue that appearance is irrelevant. If we're honest, very few of us really manage to judge people on personality alone. But feminists know that beauty is never the best way of judging whether someone is a nice person, and that 'I was beautiful once' does not hold the same currency as 'I was a good friend', 'I was nice to people' or even 'I once saved a kitten from drowning.'

Virgin or whore

I doubt many people pick up on the biblical undertones of reality TV shows like *The Bachelor*, where contestants undertake tasks in order to win dates. But perhaps the first beauty contest with a relationship as the prize is the biblical story of Esther, familiar to young Jewish girls from the retelling each year on the festival of Purim.

King Ahashuerus of Shushan in Persia commands his wife, Vashti, to dance for him and his friends. She refuses and is banished from the kingdom. Ahashuerus holds a beauty contest to find a new queen and Esther wins. The king does not know Esther is Jewish and when her cousin uncovers a plot to kill all the Jews by Haman, the King's Prime Minister, he persuades Esther to go to the king and tell him that she is Jewish and that Haman is planning to kill her people. She does this, and Haman is killed instead, on the gallows intended for the Jews.

What is a young feminist to make of this story, sitting in her Jewish Sunday school waiting impatiently for the bell to ring so she can get on with her weekend? Let's take Vashti, the queen who will not be summoned to be shown off to her husband's friends. Her refusal to dance ultimately robs her of any power she may have as queen, as she is banished from the kingdom, but at least she leaves with her dignity intact. Then there is Esther, chosen for her good looks. We never hear whether Esther is summoned to dance for the king and his friends, but as she is not banished we must assume she does comply with this kind of demand. But once in power she is not just a pretty face. She uses her influence over the king wisely, managing to avert genocide.

Is there a lesson here? The story suggests that like Esther, using feminine wiles and good looks is worth it if it gives you power to achieve things. No different from sleeping with the boss to get a promotion perhaps. She is held up as a great queen, though she is queen for no reason other than winning a beauty contest. Vashti, the first queen, who refuses to be ordered around by a man or to be treated as a sexual object, loses everything, except of course her dignity.

When it comes to Bible stories we're often presented with stark contrasts such as the virgin and the whore, a pair of images which has dogged feminism through some people's inability to see women as anything except one or the other. But of course neither Vashti nor Esther fit neatly into either category. The disgraced queen is disgraced for an act of modesty, the heroine queen has her position only through flaunting her beauty, and both seem to me to be feminists in their own way.

Noughties women are missing a trick not being familiar with this story. For they are often criticised for being attractive and sexually available and wishing to have influence and be taken seriously at the same time, with a general assumption from all sides that they have to choose one or the other. What Esther shows of course is that it's possible to do both, although my heart still goes out to Vashti who tried, and failed, to be more than just an object of desire.

Should brains always be valued over beauty?

I remember a 'Miss Wet T-Shirt' and 'Mr Wet Underpants' competition being held when I was a fresher in 1996. This isn't quite a beauty contest of course – big boobs or bulging tackle does not a beauty make. At the time I don't remember being that shocked by the event though it must have stuck in my mind because I recognised the winners for the next three years as they walked around campus and only ever thought of them by their T-shirt and underpant titles. But in retrospect I am appalled that these competitions are allowed anywhere near educational institutions, where we are tested and graded on our brains, not our physical attributes.

Antonia Strachey wrote, for the feminist website *The F Word*, about a similar competition at the London School of Economics that took place in 2007. A company called 121 Entertainment began holding beauty pageants in the various University of London colleges with the winners from each competition then going on to vie for the 'Miss University of London' title.

This went directly against the Student Union constitution that said students should not be discriminated against because of their physical appearance and the Union was forced to back out of the event. Strachey wrote:

> *Universities should aim to contribute to students' knowledge, growth and confidence. They also engage in research. These should be their two fundamental goals and their success at achieving them should be the basis of their reputation. How can a*

beauty pageant contribute? Why should a centre of learning have anything to say about the attractiveness of its students?

This is utterly true. We are snobby about beauty contests because we know that people should not get ahead based solely on their looks. I may have enjoyed the wet underpants/t-shirt competition when I was a student, but in retrospect I am horrified that I did. I am horrified also that according to Jennifer Baumgardner and Amy Richard, beauty pageants are the largest source of college scholarships in the US. Given that education changes lives more than anything else does, giving us confidence and knowledge and the skills needed to make money, why should people who win beauty contests get this opportunity more than uglier people?

But horrified as I may instinctively be, there is an alternative argument of course. Some people are born with brains that are more capable than the brains of other people. Yes of course people have to work hard to make the most of their brain, but it isn't the case that everyone has the capability to be a brain surgeon or a civil engineer. Other people are born with varying degrees of good looks, giving them the raw materials that with the right tools – nice hair and clothes for example – make them more attractive. What is it about our society that means we should value those who are born with good brains more than those born with good looks? I personally would much rather be judged by my brain than by my looks and get into university based on the former. Then again, my brain is my best asset. If my legs were perhaps I would like to be judged by them.

Size matters

I wrote a piece for the *Observer* once on being fat and happy. This is how I started it:

> *I am fat and I am happy. I hope you took notice of that, for I shall write it only once. Actually, that's not true. I like excess, it's the reason I'm fat.*

I got a huge response from fat people. One overweight man I know, high up in politics, told me he kept it pinned to his fridge. This was fat people fighting back and letting the world know that being fat is not the worst thing in the world.

Wouldn't I rather be slim you ask? Well yes, I would like to be slim, for health reasons mainly but also so I can buy nicer clothes, run faster to catch buses and live longer, but clearly, not quite as much as I would like that extra portion of chips. But the main point of my article was to show that fat people are not just victims to be pitied. I don't want people to pity me – I want people to treat me as any other person and acknowledge that I may be happy and I may be sad and neither of these are necessarily because I am overweight.

There are of course health risks associated with being fat. Fat people know this just as smokers know that they risk lung cancer and other illnesses and joggers know that they are more likely to hurt a tendon (which is why the idea of making fat people, but not joggers, pay for medical treatment infuriates me). But the real reason that feminists need to think about fat is because society particularly judges women who are overweight, assuming they are worse people by virtue of their size.

Take for example this obituary of an education adviser to the government that appeared in a national paper. Reading the obituary you can tell that she achieved a tremendous amount and was well thought of. After listing her career achievements, the obituary then says this:

> She was also universally liked. Slim, elegant, thoughtful and kind, she was economical with words, which she used precisely, alighting on exactly the word she wanted like a discriminating bird on a twig.

I'm sure she was all of these things but does the fact that she was slim really matter? Perhaps it did to her, but should the outsider reading an obituary now think of her as a better person because she was slim? What relevance does that have to her qualities as a person?

Susie Orbach wrote a famous book called *Fat is a Feminist Issue*. In it she looked at fat as not being about food itself but as being a reaction to our social situation and the way we are seen by ourselves and others. She would reject my assertion that I am fat because I choose excess over restraint and cookies over celery. Instead she says that women who are fat make themselves so in order to avoid being seen as the stereotypical perfect woman. By being fat, she says, you refuse to play along with this and thus give yourself some power and get taken more seriously as a brain rather than as a sex object. In other words you deliberately desexualise yourself in order to be more than just a woman.

I don't agree with this. I have met enough men who say that they prefer a woman with a bit of meat on her than one that is all bony. Selfishly I applaud this sentiment – it has certainly worked in my favour – but this preference does bring the argument back to what men want – cuddly women – rather than what it is women want for themselves.

The trouble with the discussion about fat, particularly in relation to women, is that it has become too generalised. So fat women are lumped together as one group, either all unhappy or all unattractive. The same goes for extremely thin women. There has been a lot of focus on size zero models in recent years, particularly following the death of two South American models after starvation diets in a bid to be size zero and the subsequent banning of models with a body mass index of less than eighteen at Madrid Fashion Week and other events. Subsequently, it has become as easy to demonise thin women as it has obese women. But whereas everybody assumes that no women would choose to be large, when it comes to size zero (the British size four), the worry is that girls see incredibly thin models and want to be like them, buying into their use by the fashion and advertising industry to equate extremely thin women with trendiness, happiness and riches.

But both of these are anti-feminist viewpoints as they see women as groups defined by their external characteristics rather than as individuals. What we need to remember is that being fat, or being thin, means nothing in itself, just as the education adviser would not have had an obituary in the national papers if slimness had been her only attribute. Size should just be a small part of our identity, and should be a small part of how others view us, even if our size is relatively big.

What's wrong with saggy arms?

It's not just fat that society doesn't like to see out and about though. There seems to be a general acceptance that there is something wrong with saggy arms. Saggy arms of course afflict the fat and the old. We can see this in the popular term for saggy arms – bingo wings – a phrase which manages to be ageist, classist and sexist all at once.

I don't know anyone who likes every part of their body. In fact there seems to be no correlation between how beautiful other people perceive you to be and how attractive you find yourself – even supermodels complain of disliking their crooked toe for example, or their mis-shaped earlobes.

The American writer Nora Ephron seems to be okay with her arms. But as the title of her book *I Feel Bad About My Neck* suggests, there is another part of her that she does not like:

> *I feel bad about my neck. Truly I do. If you saw my neck, you might feel bad about it too, but you'd probably be too polite to let on ... Every so often I read a book about age, and whoever's writing it says it's great to be old. It's great to be wise and sage and mellow ... Of course it's true that now I'm older, I'm wise*

*and sage and mellow. And it's true that I honestly do under-
stand just what matters in life. But guess what? It's my neck.*

The journalist Angela Phillips did not like Ephron's book or her
lament about her neck. Writing for the *Comment is Free* website,
she said:

> I Feel Bad About My Neck *is one long, desperate whine
> about how terribly time-consuming it is to keep an ageing body
> looking good. Ephron used to be witty, wise and interested in the
> human condition. Her book is neither witty nor wise, and
> demonstrates only an interest in herself.*

She seems to suggest that Ephron should only be musing on the
wider world, and not on her own appearance. But this is
precisely what noughties feminism rejects, knowing that we can
simultaneously be concerned about the state of the world and
the state of our eyeshadow, if we so desire.

In the same article, Phillips goes on to criticise another
journalist, Christa D'Souza, who had written for the *Observer*
about her fear of ageing and her need to continue to dress in a
young way. Phillips has found not fear, she says, but joy, in
ageing:

> *The great joy of middle age is that, by the time we have reached
> it, most of us already have a circle of friends and colleagues who
> know us for what we do, how we think, how well we cope in a
> crisis and whether or not we can be relied on for support. We
> have reached the happy stage of being known from the inside and*

not having to depend too much on how we look to signal our status. That doesn't mean we don't care about our appearance. It is just that we no longer have to use it as a flag to wave in order to attract attention to ourselves.

D'Souza should come to terms with her age, we are told, and Phillips tells her how:

The answer to Christa's problem is simple: it's time to grow up, get your hair cut shorter, and kick the miniskirts into the back of the cupboard. Then get on with enjoying the power that goes with age.

To enjoy your age you have to act your age seems to be the message here. But wait, feminism is about wearing what you want, not telling other women what to wear. Now I can't claim the moral high ground as I too have raised an eyebrow at women walking down the street in what seems to me to be inappropriate clothing be it a skirt that is fewer centimetres long than the wearer's age or an inappropriate slogan on a t-shirt. But on reflection, how dare I? We each choose the image we want to present to the world and this includes both the teenagers in goth clothing and older women in mini skirts. A feminist dresses for herself, not to conform to rules that others set. For some feminists this may be a top revealing a pert tummy and breasts. For other feminists it may be the same top revealing a flabby tummy and sagging breasts. For other feminists it may be something that covers up the tummy and breasts, whether pert or flabby or saggy, like the stereotypical feminist dungarees. And guess what, some feminists don't even think about this and just wear what they want. Therefore while Phillips might be right that D'Souza may not find dressing for her age a burden and may in fact embrace and enjoy all that it has to offer, if D'Souza wants to continue to dress in a style more typical of younger women then she should do so.

And when she no longer looks good she is allowed to lament this, as Ephron laments the loss of her wrinkle-free neck. Lamenting our changing bodies is a natural part of getting older. This doesn't mean we think less of ourselves as people, or that others should treat us differently, or that we shouldn't wear our sags and wrinkles with pride as a sign of the lives we have led, because hopefully at the same time as we lament we will also know inside that there was more to us than smooth skin anyway.

The ugly truth

Dove, the moisturiser and soap people, have an ongoing advertising campaign about 'real beauty', using pictures of 'real' women. Their first advert was personally embarrassing because one of the women, pictured in her underwear, looked quite like me, and several people commented that they'd seen me nearly naked on the back of a bus, which is only marginally better than being told you look like the back end of a bus. This would have been fine if it hadn't been in work meetings.

The Dove campaign has been praised for widening the definition of beauty, but I'm still uncomfortable with the message it is giving out in the guise of trying to give teenagers more self-esteem. Their research showed that British girls have one of the highest incidences of low self-esteem in the world, with ninety-two per cent of fifteen to seventeen year olds wanting to change something about their bodies. 'Tell them they're beautiful' is written on a board at the front of a classroom, Bart Simpson style, in one of the photographs in the campaign material.

This is a nice aim. Wouldn't it be lovely if everyone believed they were beautiful, and Dove is right, a freckly face or a plump body doesn't necessarily exclude you from this. But the campaign, which attempts to show less conventional forms of beauty, completely fails to accept the idea that some people are ugly, and more importantly, that this is okay and ugly people are just as valid as people. This isn't just a Dove thing, it's society generally and specifically an issue affecting women – I can think of many ugly men on television for example but no ugly women.

In seeking to widen the definition of beauty, Dove actually makes the situation worse for those who still don't fit it. Now that the vision of beauty isn't just an unrealistic size eight clothes hanger, but many other things too, if you don't fall into any of them you're well and truly untouchable.

If Dove really were serious about raising self-esteem rather than selling moisturiser, then it would be focusing on internal beauty such as acts of tolerance, understanding and kindness – qualities that anybody can achieve and that are worth far more than a pretty face. By placing the emphasis on widening the definition of beauty, they add to the idea that women should be judged by how they look. It is misogyny dressed up as feminism.

Dove is part of a multinational company that wants to sell its products, and we'd be foolish to expect anything other than what focus groups tell marketing managers works for them. This is fine, that's capitalism after all. But don't let them fool you into thinking they are changing the way we think about beauty. If they were doing that they wouldn't be widening the definition of beauty, but would be accepting that beauty, ugliness and everything in between, however well moisturised, is of equal worth.

Is plastic fantastic?

Is it just me who finds it amusing that the organisation for the advancement of education and practice of aesthetic plastic surgery for public benefit is called Baaps (The British Association of Aesthetic Plastic Surgeons) when changing your baps by having a boob job is the most popular procedure for women having elective surgery? Quite possibly, but then I do find jokes about willies, breasts, farts and snot rather funny.

The name is about the only funny thing about cosmetic surgery though. In 2007 32,453 surgical procedures were carried out by Baaps members and 29,572 of these were carried out on women, the most popular of which was breast augmentation. This was followed closely by eyelid surgery, face or neck lifts, liposuction and breast reduction.

I used to be dead set against cosmetic surgery. Not only is it cheating in the quest to look good which we are conditioned to think should require some sacrifice if it is to be deserved (though natural beauties make no such sacrifice), but it is conforming to an external set of rules about what looks good. I also dislike it when women pretend their changed body is all natural, refusing to admit they may have had something done. This is a huge betrayal to other women. Fair enough, you might want to change something – we do that all the time when we have a flattering hair cut or wear make-up that disguises a blemish. But to try to make other women think that your look is achievable without cheating can only contribute to feelings of inadequacy about their own bodies. Not only that but any surgical procedure carries with it a risk of going wrong and research has shown that people undergoing these operations are often not fully aware of these risks.

But I did change my mind a little when I had a student who told me she'd had a nose job when she was eighteen. She'd always hated her nose, she said, and now she didn't. She could now go out without worrying about what people thought of it and she could look in the mirror without feeling miserable. Her boyfriend had told her she didn't need it, she said, but she wasn't doing it for him but for her and what's more, it was the best thing she had ever done.

Of course it's sad that someone's nose (or breasts or eyelids or whatever) can cause them so much misery. It would be much better if we could embrace our features in all their shapes and sizes. And while it would be nice to tackle the root causes of people disliking their noses such as the prevalence of 'perfect' faces in the media, that seems unlikely to happen quickly. Which isn't to say I am suggesting people go out and have cosmetic surgery – far from it. I would rather everybody was happy with whatever bodies they have. But we don't judge hairy women having laser hair removal or grey haired women dying their hair in the same way. If cosmetic surgery really makes a difference to a woman's life, isn't it more misogynistic to prevent her from doing it?

Hair, there and everywhere

Men probably wouldn't believe it but all but the blondest of women have hair on their toes, their bellies, their nipples, their moustache area and sometimes their chin, not to mention a million other places that the odd hair can pop up unannounced, showing itself only at the worst possible moment, when undressing in front of a new lover, or when the tweezers have gone astray. Our eyebrows, believe it or not, are not naturally smooth and shaped. Our legs, unless shaved each day or waxed each fortnight, have stubble and patches of hair. And our pubes, left to live their natural lifespan, are bushy and long and wiry, poking out of knickers and bikinis and travelling several inches down our legs. I even know one woman who shaves her arms regularly in case men think she is unwomanly.

Yet an alien (always in films depicted as hairless) returning home and describing humans to their friends might say of the difference between men and women, that women usually have more hair on their head and hardly any on their bodies whereas with men it is the other way round.

Women spend a huge amount of time and money on removing hair from their bodies. It was the 1970s feminists' refusal to do this that led to the image of the angry campaigner with hairy armpits. Despite the first version of *The Joy of Sex* showing women with hairy armpits, women today have embraced the clean-shaven pit and you would be hard pressed to find many noughtie girls letting their armpit or other body hair grow naturally. So ubiquitous has the smooth pit become, that a hairy pit is now seen as the unnatural option. Remember the furore in 1999 when film star Julia Roberts, wearing a sleeveless red dress at the *Notting Hill* premiere, waved at fans and flashed her hairy pits? Or, despite the praise for her acting when Salma Hayek depicted artist Frida Kahlo, moustache and all, the discussions on how none of us would dare to do the same?

Like most areas concerning our own looks, when it comes to feminism I don't suggest there is just one way to express your beliefs. I am saddened that women have to spend so much time, money and effort removing their body hair. On the other hand, it takes a brave woman to fight the hairy fight by herself – I'm certainly not about to be the one who leads the way. To go to the swimming pool with pubes coming out of the sides of a bikini, to let facial hair be obvious rather than removed or bleached. Even if I were comfortable with it, society wouldn't be.

Toe cleavage

One of the biggest responses I've had from an article I've written came from just one small anecdote in a piece about appropriate dressing in the workplace for the *Observer*. It appeared after a news story in which a lawyer, Maxine Kelly, went to court seeking the right to wear short skirts at work.

I wrote:

> *I went to an early-evening work reception last week and worried for some time about what to wear. In the end, I went for black trousers and a green top I frequently wear for work – low but shoulders covered and not too much breast on show. I thought the outfit would show I was serious and able to network without relying on flirting.*
>
> *I thought 'Tory wife' shoes – black with a little heel and big bows – completed the ensemble pretty well until another woman said she thought the shoes were sexy. The crease between my toes peeping out from the shoes would remind men of cleavage, she assured me. It's a minefield what to wear for work events, when even toes can be construed as a come-on.*

For me the clever turn of phrase here was 'Tory wife' shoes, as I was then working for a Labour-affiliated think tank. That phrase, I thought, would conjure up images of demure women at home in the country looking after the children, baking muffins and never uttering a cross word, not even when their husbands are caught out by the tabloids in a compromising situation with a secretary. It never crossed my mind that toe cleavage was going to be the phrase that people remembered, going to show perhaps that people think about cleavage far more than they usually admit.

Toe cleavage. Urgh! It brings to mind odd fetishes and strange sexual encounters. I still own the shoes in question though I wear them with care these days. When I'm not wearing them, people come up to me at parties and enquire why I am not showing any toe cleavage. And what disturbs me even more is that now when they refer to the article and look at my feet, the phrase has become a self-fulfilling prophecy, because they will be thinking about whether or not my toes remind them of my breasts, and my breasts aren't something I necessarily want them thinking about.

The breast of times, the worst of times

A friend of mine went on television representing her organisation. Shortly afterwards, she received a letter complaining that on television she had 'displayed' her cleavage. The letter went on: 'Please cover your breasts properly. Respectable men, women and children do not want to see your cleavage. Sluttish behaviour is degrading. Have some dignity.'

Putting aside the fact that the letter writer equates cleavage with sluttish behaviour and sluttish behaviour with degradation, you would think from this that my friend had got her breasts out live on air rather than wearing a business outfit with a mere hint of cleavage.

I particularly liked this suggested response from our friend Emma however:

Dear Mr X,

I am deeply upset to have caused you distress by neglecting to don my habit before appearing on television. I was, obviously mistakenly, under the impression that I was appearing on the show by virtue of my years of experience and my position of authority on the subject being discussed. I therefore, naively, assumed that I would be judged based on what I said on the programme as opposed to what I wore. This was obviously a grave error of judgement on my part.

That said, having re-watched the programme several times I am still at a loss to recognise the indecency which was the cause of your offence. Obviously, you are in a better position than I am to recognise this as it appears that you, selflessly and at great personal risk — for which you should be commended, of course — were paying much closer attention to the particular offending area. I only hope that in this courageous undertaking you managed to avoid injury, such as eye-strain or heart problems. I did, however, see that there was showing, above my top, an area of my skin which could not reasonably be assumed to be part of my neck. Again, you see, I have failed in my duty to recognise the potential threat that this exposure poses to the moral — and probably physical and mental — health of the nation. I can only apologise unreservedly and thank you for drawing this to my attention.

I must, in fact, thank you doubly, for your message has made me aware of other dangerous items of clothing in my wardrobe. I am embarrassed to admit that just the other day I left the house – on some errand or other, possibly to buy a cookery book or a copy of Good Housekeeping, *I can't remember – in a skirt which finished above my knees! I shudder at what, in my ignorance, I might have caused with such an outwardly sluttish act. I can only be thankful that I didn't encounter anyone with a heart condition who could have been shocked into an early grave by my depravity. Or, worse still, a child who could have been morally bankrupted by the sight and whom I may have set irrevocably onto a life of criminality and hopelessness. I am also thankful that I didn't get what I obviously deserved – forced into an alley and raped by some man whose sense of decency and propriety had been forced out of him by the sight of my bare knees. It would have been all my own fault as I obviously would have been asking for it, and, let's face it, I probably would have enjoyed it really.*

Anyway, again I thank you for your vigilance and your warning. Too often when I appear on TV people are merely paying attention to the words coming out of my mouth and are not concentrating on the obvious depravity and sluttishness which is occurring below my neck. Your guidance and reflections are, of course, greatly appreciated. Please do, whenever you see me on TV in the future, pay special attention to my breasts – I rely on you to put me right when my underlying whore-ish nature (which is every woman's curse, of course) gets the better of me.

Yours in gratitude …

The vital organ

When I was planning this book I wrote an outline of what each chapter would be about and a line or two on the essence of my argument. *The Vagina Monologues* was the chapter heading for this section, and the note just read 'and why it is a load of bollocks'. Which is ironic really because bollocks is exactly what it isn't. When it comes to *The Vagina Monologues*, bollocks are out and the fanny is in.

For the uninitiated, *The Vagina Monologues* by Eve Ensler is a play made up of a series of monologues, each relating the vagina. So for example one is about a woman's first period, another about rape as a war crime in Bosnia, another about sexual abuse and another about a dominatrix.

Ensler wrote the play, she says, to 'celebrate the vagina'. This has morphed in the years since it was first performed in 1996 to being part of a campaign to end violence against women. At the end of the 1990s, V-Day was created, a day of women's awareness with the aim of ending violence against women. Often a performance of *The Vagina Monologues* also takes place.

I still shudder to think about the time I went, early in the noughties, with three friends to a production of *The Vagina Monologues in London*, starring its author, Ensler. At one point in the play, having listened to many musings on vaginas, the women in the audience are asked to stand up and chant the word cunt in unison. We did it, my friends and I, but it was not a pleasant experience. Chanting the word cunt does not a feminist make. This is not because I am uncomfortable with the word cunt (see chapter 2 for my views on this) but because bringing women's experiences down solely to the vagina is to belittle the cause of women everywhere. We are more than our vaginas. I am not the kind of person who is that happy standing up in a group and chanting any word, but if I have to do it and that word has to represent modern women and our lack of shame about who we are, I would prefer to chant the word 'brain' over and over rather than 'cunt'.

Knickers to you

I watch the television programme *How To Look Good Naked*. The presenter, an openly gay man, tries each week to help a shy, under-confident woman become so comfortable with her body that she can walk down a catwalk in underwear or pose nude for a picture.

This is not necessarily a bad aim in itself. I appeared naked except for body paint in *The Sunday Times* for an article, and stripped off for a life drawing class for another article. Despite having a rather large and far from perfect body, nudity does not faze me too much. In fact, one of the reasons I was happy to do these things was to prove, to myself and others, that body confidence isn't about having the perfect body. So while I applaud the show's aim of giving women confidence about their bodies, I am not so sure about some of the messages it sends out.

For example, there's always a point in the show where the presenter goes through the wardrobe of the woman being featured in that episode, making her throw away unflattering clothes, even if they are old favourites. Sometimes he gets to the underwear drawer and seizes on the comfy greying plain cotton knickers and exclaims over their lack of sexiness. In one episode I watched he actually put this woman's knickers in the shredder to show his point. 'How are you ever going to look sexy in that?' he asked her.

Er, excuse me. Knickers are not for looking sexy. Well, sexy knickers are for looking sexy, or making you feel sexy, at a time of sexiness appropriate to the wearer's choosing. But primarily knickers are meant to be comfortable. Their everyday role is fourfold; to keep our outer clothes clean from any bodily secretions, to support our bodies, to prevent our most sensitive areas from being irritated by the rough material of outer clothing and to prevent our pubes from getting caught in zips (yes, whatever, we're meant to wax them all off, I forgot).

This programme was suggesting that a woman has to be sexy at all times and that the only knickers allowed in her drawers are sexy ones. Now putting aside whether it is only the lacy little numbers that are sexy (think Bridget Jones's oversized knickers and the reaction they provoke), this reduces the role of women down to being a sex object. There is no discussion of what underwear is functional, or comfortable. No, telling women to only wear sexy clothes, knickers or otherwise, is to say they are worth more if they are sexy, the exact opposite of what feminism is about, and although ostensibly about giving one woman confidence, it is a huge knock to the women's movement as a whole.

The sound of silence

Do you ever walk past a building site and feel disappointed when you're not whistled at? I know this is not what a feminist should say, but I do feel rather disappointed when I am in a situation where traditionally men are supposed to fancy any woman who walks past, and I don't hear a peep.

The thing is, though we shouldn't have to be whistled at or acknowledged by men to feel validated, sometimes that is exactly what we need, a confidence boost that lets us know we are attractive.

Whoa, you may think, you thought I was arguing elsewhere that ugliness is as worthy as prettiness, that what we look like shouldn't matter, and that the emphasis on women to be sexy undermines the whole movement. And of course all that is true. But the typical noughtie girl feminist is torn in many ways. She knows on the one hand that looks don't matter. On the other hand she knows that she wants to feel attractive and that she wants this to be confirmed by other people. No wonder many people don't understand feminism – it is a mass of contradictions.

The thing is of course, that when builders do whistle, I am the first to turn around and yell at them for turning me into a sexual object when I am just getting on with my day and to get on with their work and leave women alone. Only I don't of course, I do that most British of expressions of disgust, and quietly tut, while at the same time being secretly pleased to have been noticed.

Time of the month

I rather like the biblical idea of women on their period needing some time alone and being sent to a separate tent. After all, the time of the month is exactly when we need some space to relax, look after ourselves and wallow in the pain of our insides dripping out.

But while I believe that women need space and understanding while they are on their period, I hugely resent the men who feel they can bandy around the letters PMS as a response to any women disagreeing with them.

I mean, isn't it funny how men never want to talk about the details of periods – you know, the way the blobby bits come out, the constipation, the spots and the general ickiness, but they love suggesting it as a reason for you not doing what they want you to do.

There are of course extreme cases of PMS in which irritability and aggression can have a huge impact on a woman's life. There are even cases where it has been put forward as a defence for murder. But for the vast majority of women PMS is not something that impacts on their day-to-day life. Just like a man, we may be emotional or touchy without a physiological reason, but just because that is the mood we are in. Is it unreasonable to suggest that I shove a tampon up the penis of the next man who suggests PMS as a reason for me disagreeing with him, and see how he likes blood coming out of his most intimate hole?

7

How not to be a domestic goddess

I know some people who actually enjoy cleaning. They see it as therapeutic and they like the glow they get after polishing or scrubbing or scraping. I don't feel like that about cleaning but I do like cooking – I like mixing and whisking and spooning and tasting. But being a noughtie girl has nothing to do with whether you like domestic tasks and everything to do with whether you have to do them. I enjoy spending time in the kitchen, but if I had to cook all of the meals in my household I would start to feel somewhat put upon. I don't enjoy cleaning, but if I did none at all and my partner did everything (he doesn't) then how would I be able to feel I had an equal relationship?

Noughtie girls and their partners recognise that equality means splitting all the tasks life throws at them, whether enjoyable or not. In theory at least, a noughtie girl does not leave all the driving to her male partner, nor does she protest that she cannot read maps. Her partner does not leave her to write the Christmas cards or lay claim to ownership of the garden shed. In practice of course every relationship works differently, and we have to recognise that.

I like this example from the 1975 novel *The History Man* by Malcolm Bradbury in which the main couple, Howard and Barbara Kirk, have a rather dysfunctional marriage. Nonetheless, they do divide up the day-to-day tasks such as here where they are organising a party:

> *And so Howard talks on the telephone, and makes twenty-five calls, while Barbara sits in the canvas chair; and then Barbara talks on the telephone, and makes twenty-five calls, while Howard sits in the canvas chair. The Kirks are a modern couple, and believe in dividing all tasks equally down the middle, half for you, half for me like splitting an orange, so that both get involved and neither gets exploited. When they have finished on the telephone they sit in the canvas chairs again, and Barbara says, 'You buy the drinks, I'll buy the food.' And the party is all ready.*

I like to think I am in some ways a little bit of a domestic goddess. Sure I leave my dirty knickers on the floor and never clean the bath, but I do make a great chocolate cake and I am quite good at choosing birthday cards. But choosing not to be a domestic goddess isn't about how good we are at individual tasks but about our refusal to be the one who does them all the time, and our refusal to do what goddesses throughout mythology do, and make their tasks look effortless.

I will not wash my partner's pants

One Christmas when I was very small, around five or six, I was given a toy washing machine by my grandparents. This might not sound like a great present but I loved it. Using real soap and water, the washing machine went through a genuine cycle and really cleaned things. My grandpa let me use some of his handkerchiefs to practise on. I don't remember ever wondering why I got this present and not my brother.

Zoom forward twenty-five years and I have lost my enthusiasm for washing. It is one of my least favourite chores. But much as I love Katharine Whitehorn's quotation from a 1963 article she wrote for the *Observer* – 'Have you ever taken anything back out of the dirty-clothes basket because it had become, relatively, the cleaner thing?' – I understand that unless I want people to give me a very wide berth when I go out in clothes stained and smelly from previous wearings, washing clothes is a chore that has to be done. Nevertheless, grotty job or not, I don't expect anyone else to have to root around a washing basket full of my dirty knickers and return them to me clean. Similarly I don't want to do this for any other adults.

I presumed everyone thought like this. So it was a surprise when in a discussion with my friends about washing one day (and really, can you imagine any groups of men going to the pub and discussing washing?), it came out that many of my girl friends do all the laundry in their relationships. This isn't just a case of putting their own clothes in the machine and adding a few of their partner's clothes to make it a full load. No, they do all of it. It's easier, they said, than nagging their partner to do it himself, and that if they waited for him to do the washing they would never have any clean clothes.

There is a simple solution to this of course – separate washing baskets. Because if there's one thing I won't do in a relationship, it is wash my partner's pants.

My partner thinks this is ridiculous. He wants all the washing to be in one basket and for us to each put a wash on, as and when required, with both of our clothes. But I think it's degrading. I don't want to sift through someone else's pants turning them the right way out and deciding whether they need a light wash or an environmentally unfriendly kill all known germs sixty degree wash. I don't really want to do it to my own knickers, and your own knickers are less offensive than other people's pants.

But at the core of this argument is not whether you want to touch someone else's smalls, but the division of domestic labour in the home generally. Research earlier this decade found that women still take responsibility for most of the housework despite being more likely than ever before to be in paid employment and despite the cultural trend of the 'new man'. Even women who earn more than their partners and are in successful time-consuming jobs come home and do double the amount of housework their partners do. Believe it or not, this isn't because women like doing housework.

In my household things generally stay messy until one of us can bear it no longer and starts to clean up or tidy away. This might be me, or it might be him, but I am almost certain that the reason it is not always me is because of the stance I took from the beginning about not washing his pants.

Sharing the shitty jobs

I think it is safe to say I am not the most house-proud of people, preferring a cosy film of dirt to sparkling surfaces (unless someone else has made them sparkle). In fact Sarah, my best friend who I lived with for four years in my early twenties, once wondered aloud how long it would take me to get round to cleaning the bathroom if she didn't do it. When I lived alone I found out – two and a half years!

But sometimes you just have to bite the bullet and clean – when your in-laws are coming over for example, or when the television documentary on flesh eating bacteria starts to worry you. When this time comes though, even when there is a division of labour in the home where you both take responsibility for cleaning, how many of you have ever seen a man volunteer to clean the loo?

When we moved in together, my man said to me that he is happy to do most chores, but he hates cleaning the loo. Guess what I told him, possibly angrily with my eyes flashing and a red mist descending in my head. Yes, that's right, I don't much like it either. Just as I will not wash his pants, I will not clean the germs from his shit more times than he does mine.

Is there a solution to this? Well some couples I know tell me proudly that they are equal because neither of them does any house work. Instead they pay for a cleaner to come round to their house. There are of course arguments for distributing money to those who need it. Not to hire cleaners is to deny a whole raft of women the opportunity to do local flexible part time work. Nevertheless from a feminist perspective what bothers me is that when people hire a cleaner the cleaner is nearly always a woman and whichever way you look at it cleaning in the home is still seen as a woman's job, even if you are paying someone else to do it for you.

Remember the furore about tuna fishing nets catching dolphins in them? Then we all had to buy dolphin friendly tuna. I had a joke about buying tuna friendly tuna. It's called dolphin. I was reminded of that when I started thinking about all the adverts on television for cleaning products to make women's lives easier. Washing up liquid that leaves your hands feeling soft, window cleaner that just glides on, sprays that cut through grease or fizz away limescale. All intended to make women's lives easier. I tell you what would be women friendly cleaning. Men bloody doing some of it.

Other forms of labour
Of course domestic labour isn't just about cleaning the loo or doing the laundry. There are plenty of other forms of domestic labour that largely fall to women.

Take organising your social life for example. Those of you who live with a male partner – how many times does he organise having people round for supper and do the shopping for it, the cooking and the tidying up afterwards? (Unless it's a barbecue of course, then just try wresting away the tongs to cook a steak. Nope, men do meat.)

What about interior design? Do your menfolk ever buy the cushions or choose the curtains? How about photo albums? Men may enjoy playing with the digital settings on the camera, but how often do they choose the best shots, arrange them in an album and write the labels saying who is who?

What about greetings cards? Would people get greetings at Christmas or thank you notes without women writing and sending them? As one woman said to me: 'For the last twenty-five years I have been sending cards to people my husband knew at university and I've never even met them. He still insists they are kept on the list though – not that he as much as signs his name.'

The same goes for writing postcards while on holiday and remembering birthdays. In fact in many homes it seems that women do pretty much everything that is pretty, fluffy or edible.

To be fair, this is not something men make us do. It is something we tend to choose to do ourselves. That's why it's not as easy as saying that where there is a man in the house he must take equal responsibility for this kind of task. Because the thing is, often women don't want to give up roles which traditionally belong to women.

Think about your home. Would you be happy for your partner to decide what colour the walls are painted? What if he wanted to cook every single night in 'your' kitchen? Or if you never got to browse the supermarket shelves and decide what you want to buy. See, we pretend we want to share these responsibilities but there are many areas in the home in which we want to be the ones to make the decisions. We may, I fear, have to let some of this power go, if we are to argue successfully for equality.

In the meantime though, would it matter if we just stopped? If we didn't buy cushions, choose new wallpaper, send birthday cards, have dinner parties, buy Christmas presents or organise our photos? I mean apart from the fact our sofas would be uncomfortable, we'd have old wallpaper on our walls, no post on our own birthdays, more nights alone in front of the telly, piles of loose photos and none of the joy of buying (or receiving, once people cottoned on) presents. It might not matter in the wider scheme of things but it's not fluffy or girlie to say this isn't how I want my life to be, and that I don't want to be the one doing it all.

A decision I made all by myself

Hello,

Someone from your company rang me today in response to a call for quotations I put out for companies to quote for making a window into a door at my property. They were very polite on the

*phone and suggested someone come over to give me an estimate
tomorrow at 10am.*

*This evening the person who was supposed to be coming over
to give me the estimate rang to confirm this appointment and
to get some extra details. He asked whether my husband
would be home – in fact he has no idea whether or not I am
married, and said he would like both me and my partner to be
there when he came round. I have several problems with this.
First, it is the customer, not the firm, who decides who is there
when you estimate. Second, how dare you assume that people
can only make decisions when their husband is there. And third,
do not make assumptions over whether or not someone has a
husband.*

*I informed this caller that I have authority to make decisions
myself and he said he would give me a sale price when he visited
that would only be available there and then if I made a decision.
I said that would not happen and he asked if that was because I
had to discuss it with my husband and said that's why he
wanted to see us both. I explained that I like time to think about
decisions and to compare quotes and to think about how things
fit into our general scheme of work. Your salesman started to put
pressure on me and said that's why he likes to see people with
their husbands – bear in mind he still had no idea of my marital
status at this time. I told him that my partner and I would never
make a decision on the spot, regardless of whether we see people
together or alone.*

I ended up cancelling my appointment as I was offended and

upset by the hard sell before even having met anyone from your
company and from your company's sexist assumptions.

I look forward to receiving your response.

Regards,

Ellie Levenson

Having your cake and eating it

The slow food movement, the antidote to fast food, is becoming increasingly popular as our interest in organic produce and healthy eating has grown over the past few years. Slow food doesn't necessarily have to be cooked slowly. Rather the emphasis is on ensuring regional dishes remain in our consciousness and food is something we enjoy as a group and with thought. This all sounds lovely – I am for it wherever possible.

But let us not forget that one of the biggest steps forward for feminism in the Western world, possibly bigger than getting the vote, bigger than the Equal Pay Act and bigger than maternity leave, was the invention of the ready meal. In much the same way as lifts needed to be invented before skyscrapers became a practical proposal, for women to get into the workplace and stake their claim to equality we needed help ensuring our families had food on the table even if we didn't have huge amounts of time to prepare it. In this respect convenience food has been a great thing.

I do know men who cook. My partner is one of them. But anecdotally I also know many households where men do none of the week in week out drudgery of cooking daily for the family – the constant grind of unexciting meals that nevertheless need cooking to ensure everyone is warm and well fed. Then they cook something flamboyant for a dinner party and get all the buzz and joy of acclaim that comes from cooking something fancy for other people and a reputation as a man who cooks. That is not sharing the cooking. That is showing off.

Joanna Moorhead wrote a brilliant piece in the *Guardian* in January 2007 in which she praised convenience foods. Moorhead does not like cooking. She starts with a rather scary statistic:

> *Last week, to my horror, I found out that I can expect to do one of my least favourite activities about 45,990 times over the course of my lifetime. That is the equivalent of an hour a day, or seventeen days a year, or, perhaps most alarmingly, almost three years in all.*

But most interestingly she points to a by-product of our current penchant for organic food.

> *Today in my corner of south-west London – and far, far beyond, I suspect – you would be a social pariah if you dared invite anyone else's children over and fed them something less than an organic, sugar-free, home-cooked gastro experience without a trans fat in sight … Clearly fresh, nutritious family meals are a good thing, but if there has been a loser in the Jamie Oliver children's food revolution, it has surely been your average mother, now*

burdened not merely with providing meals for the whole house-hold, but also with ensuring dishes are additive-free, locally sourced, non-GM, low-fat, sugarless and made from food that comes wrapped in biodegradable packaging (if wrapped at all).

Now I'm not advocating feeding children, or adults, food that is bad for you. But it is true there is something anti-feminist about the current vogue for slow food and organic food. It's all very well taking time over cooking, but if you have a full time job, childcare commitments and other caring roles, then that is not always possible, let alone affordable. In fact the organo-fascist movement in which we expect people, usually women, to ensure food lives up to stringent standards, can be seen as a case of the anti-feminists having their organic cake and eating it, by using the need for organic food and slow food as a stick to beat women with.

Which is why I, and other noughtie girls, should not feel guilty about the occasional use of a jar of ready-made sauce or shop bought dessert.

A running away fund?

Feminists used to talk about the need for a running away fund, so that if things got too unbearable in their marriages they could take the money they had squirrelled away and run off.

This might seem like a good idea in principle, but if you share your finances, how can you squirrel enough away to have a decent running away fund without lying to your partner? After all, what would you need? Well even for a woman without children you would need a couple of month's rent and a deposit. You would need money for food and, if you couldn't take any with you, money for clothes as well as money for bills and money for emergencies. Let's say that at the very least you need a few thousand pounds. Now hands up who has a secret stash of this much? I certainly don't. What's more, I would be rather annoyed if my partner had this much hidden away that I didn't know about. Our partnership depends on sharing what we have and prioritising our money together.

In Jenni Russell's brilliant series of articles on modern relationships published in the *Guardian* in 2005, she looked at the case study of Annabel and Henry:

> *Annabel, 38, worked as a teacher before she had children. Now she does occasional part-time work for education websites, earns around £7,000 a year and has less than £3,000 left over after paying tax and the au pair's wages. Henry gives her an allowance of £2,000 a year … Henry pays the mortgages, runs the cars, buys his brogues from Church's and his shirts from Jermyn Street, takes taxis with abandon and has a thorough knowledge of the City's finest restaurants. He spends his money as he pleases, and when he's feeling particularly generous, he allows Annabel to spend a little too. And Henry's explanation: 'I work bloody hard for my money. Annabel chose to give up her career. I keep the show on the road – if she wants to do what I do, she's welcome to try.'*

I remember reading this article when it was published and sending it to several of my friends, many of whom were in new but serious relationships and deciding how to arrange their finances. What shocked me wasn't just Henry's callous disregard for the inequality in their life, but the fact that they don't share their money at all. In the same article Russell quoted the case of another couple where the male half bought himself a theatre ticket but not one for his wife who couldn't afford it.

It is vitally important for feminists not to be dependent on money from a man, not least because money is so bound up with power that if we have no money of our own we have no power of our own. But also it is not feminist to have more money than our partner, because feminism is about equality. This means recognising that whoever earns more, we play an equal role in our relationship, and that all work, whether paid employment or domestic work, is of equal value.

Sharing money doesn't work for everyone. A friend of mine says that I mustn't underestimate the importance to her, and other women, of being able to buy a pair of shoes (insert other item here if you prefer bags, or books, or whatever) on a whim without dipping into the joint pot or needing to run your decision by your partner. She sees sharing money as being anti-feminist because she equates it with giving up your independence.

It is true that you have to decide which is more important to you – the concept of your work, paid and domestic, being equal to your partners no matter how much money you are actually paid, or the importance of keeping exactly what you earn to spend as you please. For me it's the former, but for other noughtie girls it may well be the latter.

Whichever way you see it, rather than having a running away fund, what noughtie girls must to do is ensure that they have equal access to their money. This doesn't just include managing the accounts and having the relevant usernames and passwords, but also having experience of managing money. It is vital that noughtie girls know how to operate a bank account, how to apply for loans and how to budget. Noughtie girls need to have a credit rating and not be afraid of the jargon associated with processes such as applying for a mortgage or signing a contract.

This applies to single women as much as women who may share their finances with a partner, for this money savvyness means knowing how to operate independently if we need to, be it because of a break-up, widowhood or just because as equal women we want to be in control.

So no, I do not have a running away fund. But I do have running away know-how which means should I ever need to, I am financially literate. It's a running away fund of knowledge I suppose, and one we should all have.

8

Love and marriage

I've never been anti-love but I always used to be anti-marriage. It is an outdated concept, I told anyone who would listen, a piece of paper only. A relationship should be a contract renewable every day, not something you sign up to when in the first flushes of love having to then deal with the consequences of your actions every day for the rest of your life, or until the decree nisi comes through. And how, I would exclaim, can you hope to be the same person in ten or twenty years time as you are now? How can you promise to love someone forever when they might change, or you might change, or in the natural course of things you might grow apart?

A former colleague of mine, married, told me she had felt the same. 'I didn't believe in marriage,' she said 'until I met the man

I wanted to marry.' The same happened to me. In just a few months I went from being vehemently anti-marriage to being happily married. Why did I do this? It certainly wasn't because, as one friend put it, she always felt a bit guilty having sex before she was married. I can say hand on heart I have never felt guilty for having sex. Nor was it because I had always dreamed of my wedding day the way some girls do – I hadn't picked out my dress and cake in my head as a child and fantasised about the day it would come true. Nor were there religious considerations. No, I got married because I fell in love and we just wanted to.

Traditionally feminism and marriage are not necessarily seen as compatible. A woman I know who was involved with the feminist movement in the 1970s and 1980s did not marry her partner, the father of her children, both because she did not see the need to and because getting married was, to her, an anti-feminist statement. She shocked everyone who knew her, including herself, when she got married to a new partner in the noughties. Why? 'I just wanted to' she said. Which seems as good a reason as any, and providing no one else is getting hurt, the best reason for feminists to do anything, be it decide to get married, or decide not to.

Ringing the changes

I loved my engagement ring. It had been my grandma's and I felt it connected me to her. Plus it was sparkly, and it let everyone who saw me know I was getting married soon. Oh how I loved my engagement ring.

I recognise the ridiculousness of this of course. Why should I have cared whether people knew I had a partner or not, or that we planned to get married? Other than if trying to get me into bed, and even then I would expect some form of conversation first which would establish facts such as whether we were single and whether we wanted to sleep with each other (as a bare minimum!), my relationship status should be of no concern to strangers.

Yet I loved my engagement ring. I would sit on the train looking at the ring fingers of other women to see whether they too had one. How lucky I was, to be part of this club, I thought, and would exchange small smiles with other women when we clocked each other's rings.

Please understand, this is not a materialistic view – I care not for the carat, the clarity, the cut or the sheer sparkliness of other people's rings. I wasn't comparing the size of rocks or how much the ring was worth.

No, it was more basic than that. I just wanted people to realise that I had found someone who was prepared to love me forever, or to try their best to honour this commitment anyway. I may have left the house without time to sort out my hair, find clean clothes or make myself look nice, but the people on the train wouldn't be looking at me thinking 'what a mess' I thought, they would be looking at me thinking 'someone loves her'.

I am not sure that being engaged meant the same to the person I was engaged to. He knew that we were going to get married, and I knew he'd given this due consideration since he had proposed, but the period in the run up to the wedding was not, I don't think, a different state of being for him the way it was for me.

I wonder if it would have been had he had an engagement ring? When I think about why I liked my ring, I am ashamed of the anti-feminism of it all. I loved other women knowing I was loved, and other men knowing I was taken. Did I care that my husband to be did not have a ring to show he was taken also? No, because if I did not trust him to be faithful then I would not have been getting married to him in the first place, so it's not about preventing him from cheating. Besides, rings can be taken off.

So why don't men have engagement rings? I don't hold truck with the argument that men are trying to appear single until the last possible moment as I believe men who get married want to do so. After all, if you can't persuade a man to clean the loo against his will, how on earth would you persuade a man to go through all that a wedding involves against his will? No, men get married more than willingly.

Is it because women believe they should be bought something, perhaps for financial security, to ensure that having made such a financial commitment, their man will not then leave them? Maybe, though in my case my ring was a family ring so that doesn't hold true for us.

No, I think it is because women want the rest of the world to see that they are engaged, because however feminist we are, however scornful of marriage we are and however much we pretend we don't care what others think, actually we enjoy the attention. After all, I once heard someone say that there are only two times women are the centre of attention in their lives – when they are engaged and when they are pregnant.

It is easy to make the sweeping statement as a feminist that it shouldn't matter what anyone else thinks or recognises and that there is no need for rings because the marriage contract is between two individuals only. But we live in a society and it is pretty individualistic to say that who you are in a relationship with and the type of relationship you have has no impact on this society. For example, when you are married you do put the welfare of your spouse above all others, you are obligated to and have publicly promised you will. There are probably many lonely people in the vicinity of my house who could do with some company, but I spend most evenings with my spouse and we keep each other company.

This is not to say that others should be able to tell you how to live or who to love, but that unless you are hermits living in a self-sufficient hut miles from anywhere, then your relationship is in part the business of those around you. Engagement rings may be about security and about showing others you are soon to be married – perhaps if we were more confident about this as women we could do away with them, but wedding rings show your place in society, which is, whatever traditional feminist viewpoints of marriage say, neither better nor worse, but different.

A decent proposal

I say above that my husband proposed to me. I don't mean this in the strictest sense. I am a feminist – I was never going to just wait for him to pop the question. Our decision to get married was, naturally, a mutual decision borne out of discussions about our future. But once we had decided that we would get married, and even decided on the date and venue, I still wanted an official proposal. Why is this? Well I am an enthusiastic person. Sometimes I get carried away. What if, I thought, he had just mentioned marriage in passing, without really meaning it, and I had seized on it and assumed he meant it? What if I had carried him along with my enthusiasm to a point where he felt unable to back out? Sure, it was a mutual discussion, but I was the one making it happen, ringing venues to see what dates were available, planning the details of the day.

So we agreed to get married and then I said I would like a proposal, something he had gone away and planned, something that let me know he had thought about marriage and decided by himself that yes, it was something he wanted to do rather than something that had happened because my enthusiasm carried us away after a short conversation about it. So even with the venue booked and deposit paid, I didn't consider us engaged.

He went away, thought about things and planned a proposal, and even though I knew we were getting married, even though we'd had a discussion and even though we'd paid a deposit to the venue, I was a little surprised when he asked me to marry him.

I know why I wanted a proposal, I needed reassurance that I wasn't browbeating my partner into marrying me, because my personality is, at best, a rather forceful one. But why is it that in heterosexual relationships the man is expected to propose rather than the woman?

A Spanish man I know once expressed surprise to me on the British and American way of doing things. He said: 'In Spain the woman says to the man "I want to get married" and the man says "okay".' Perhaps he was joking a little, but I think this is also rather representative of what happens here. For although men tend to formally propose in the UK (I do know some women who have proposed, but they are the rarity), I think it is very unusual for this to come out of the blue, but rather after hints, discussions or full blown arguments about the future.

So rather than marriage being the man's idea, what we have is just a nationwide pretence that it is men who make the decisions about the future. And although married women may know that the decision to get married was not made for them and that the actual popping of the question was the result of a mutual dance of discussions about the future, I can't help but feel that this pretence that it is the man's role to suggest marriage does not give young girls great ideas about having an equal place in society.

The rise of the Fumbies

One thing I was sure of regarding marriage was that in no circumstances would my dad ever be asked for permission to marry me. In fact this was a tradition I thought had gone out with the ark. I don't ask my dad whether I should sleep with someone, how to spend my money or who I should be friends with – so why should he have a say in whether I should get married?

I just assumed everyone I knew felt the same about this, and certainly that the people I knew who called themselves feminists did. So when my friends started to announce their engagements, I naturally enjoyed hearing the details. I wanted to know how the proposal happened, what the ring was like, when they planned the big day to be. And then in the course of giving the details, she would say something like 'He asked my dad when I was in the loo last time we saw them' or, 'He went to see my parents and asked them by himself last weekend when I was shopping.' And worse, the woman wasn't furious that she'd been undermined in this way, she wasn't annoyed her parents had wind of an important event in her life before she did, she wasn't irritated by the lack of backbone her partner was showing. No, she was delighted at the 'respect' shown to her family (though by asking permission from anyone but her, no respect was shown to her of course).

Even more shocking was that these were women who either called themselves feminist, or who were so independent that I just assumed they were feminists. Many of them lived alone. They were financially independent. They had high-flying, difficult jobs.

Yet the minute the marriage word was mentioned, they lost their feminist instincts. Dads were being asked to give them

155

away. White dresses, traditionally symbols of virginity, were being bought. Surnames were being changed. Men were making the speeches.

I've coined a phrase for these women. They are Fumbies – that is, Feminist Until Matrimony Beckons. Fumbies think they are independent women, able to make their own decisions and speak for themselves. But on their wedding day they sit there smiling as their father and their husband speak for them. They may be grown women but they spent the night alone in their parents' house on the eve of their wedding and were then given away by their dad to their future husband. They have had sexual experiences for many years, but they think it is okay to collude in the idea that brides should be virginal by wearing white dresses. They make their own decisions in life except for one of the biggest decisions of them all when they want their partner to check that their parents have no objections.

Of course in many cases it might not just be tradition that is the incentive to ask daddy. As one soon-to-be-married male friend said to me: 'You'd have asked too if you wanted her dad to foot the bill.' I think this is pretty horrendous – both the idea that you would play the game in such a way and the idea that any financial gift would be dependent on being asked permission. Another friend of mine thought he was being feminist by asking both the bride's mother and her father, rather than just the father. This still of course takes power away from the bride. However, he did it as a mark of respect he said. So I asked him what he would have done if the parents had said no, to which he replied that he would have proposed to his girlfriend anyway. So whatever he thinks, it's clearly not about respect, as ignoring a no and asking anyway is pretty disrespectful.

I wrote an article about this in the *Guardian* in 2007 in which I quoted my dad at the end of the piece. Perhaps his attitude explains why it was inevitable I would grow up to proudly call myself a feminist.

> *My dad is lovely. He is a kind, intelligent man, and I am sure we have the same outlook on most things. But the idea that he would have any say whatsoever in my major life decisions distresses me. I can't remember me asking him permission for anything since I was about fourteen. 'I would refuse permission to any bloke who is wimpish enough to feel he has to ask me,' he says. 'And if he took any notice of me I'd think even worse of him.'*

The marriage contract

I know a woman who promised to obey her husband. An old woman you must be thinking, maybe one married at the end of the Edwardian period now nearing her hundredth birthday. Or a foreign woman from a country less enlightened than ours, or who didn't speak English well but got married here, and who didn't quite realise what she was saying. No, none of those. She is a woman born in the late seventies, a woman who went to university and got an education, a woman who has a promising career as a doctor ahead of her. She is the ideal candidate for being a noughtie girl. But guess what, she actually promised to obey her husband.

I asked her about this. She said that he promised to look after her and that included asking her opinion and taking account of that, but that there are times when a decision has to be made and she is okay with the fact that she has effectively given him permission to make those decisions and to do what he says.

I wonder how far this promise goes. If they want to watch different programmes on the television, does she obey his wish and pass him the remote control? She probably does, for obedience is effectively the relinquishment of control and she probably never got to touch the remote control in the first place. What about if he wants something other than what she has planned for dinner, for presumably she does the cooking? Does she throw away one set of ingredients and buy another? They have a child now. When she disagrees with her husband over a matter of discipline or whether the child can have more sweets, who makes the final decision?

In all relationships of course there is bound to be disagreement, and sometimes one party has to make a decision or there is stalemate. But to offer on your wedding day for that to always be the other party? Reader, it angers me.

I may have said in other parts of this book that feminism is about not judging other women, that noughtie girls can live their lives as a mass of contradictions and we must let each woman live as she wishes. Well I didn't mean it. You can judge and indeed you must judge. For those who promise to obey not just let themselves down but their whole gender.

The MRS (Hons) degree

It was often said of women who went to university that while men went to get their BA or MSc, women went to get their MRS degree, that is, to find a husband. This doesn't really hold true any more, what with people getting married later – 2006 statistics show the average age for a woman to get married for the first time was 29.7 years and for men 31.8 years.

But women do spend a lot of time searching for a man and I don't think this is necessarily a bad thing, although depending on what the individual wants this doesn't have to be marriage of course. Women do after all have a time limit on reproduction. We need to find a partner while we are relatively young, and need to start this search early in order to test out people and discard them if they are not right (or be discarded ourselves). Reproduction isn't the only reason we want a partner of course. It is not anti-feminist to admit that life is nicer when it is shared with someone. You have someone to share your interests, and to open your eyes to theirs. Someone to go to events with, someone to cuddle and someone to talk to. When you have a good partnership you feel like it is you and them against the world – there will always be someone on your side.

I remember the sheer relief, once I found a partner, of not having to look for one any more. It wasn't that I let myself go – I didn't suddenly change from going to parties in nice clothes and washed hair to wearing dirty rags and being unkempt. But it did mean I no longer had to be constantly witty and interesting, constantly flirting or wondering, when I met a new man, whether he was single, whether I liked him and whether he might like me. I didn't have to ensure I was available in case I was asked on a date, and wonder which of my bad habits to hide.

Sometimes women are criticised for trying hard to catch a man. I'm not saying that life without a partner is worthless, or that we should have a partner at any cost, but given that for many of us partnership is so pleasant, why shouldn't we do all that we can to get one?

Screwing the bastards

That women as well as men can initiate a divorce is an important part of feminism. No one, male or female, should be forced to stay in a marriage they no longer wish to be in. But the way the media sees divorcing women, portraying them as being out to wring every penny possible from their ex, is pretty unhelpful to feminists. I had thought that this was a media construct, but shortly before I bought a house with the man I was about to marry, I saw a lawyer. While we very much hoped we would to stay together, we wanted to ensure that if we did split up after a short while we would both take out of the house the amount of money we put in.

I explained to my lawyer, a woman, what we wanted. 'You could get more out of him than that' she said. I didn't want to I explained but she was insistent. I should cover my back she said, and ensure I got every penny out of him. Screw the bastard was the subtext – perhaps she was more used to dealing with people in the throes of divorce than coming to see her pre-marriage.

Divorce is sad, of course it is, even in situations where both parties want a divorce and there is no animosity. But it doesn't help women that divorce is viewed as a chance for us to get every penny we can out of the man we are divorcing.

The post-nuptial agreement

Contrary to my lawyer's advice, it's not a pre-nup that women should want however, it's a post-nup, a statement of how each party will behave after marriage. If I could have written a post-nup it would have included an agreement to equally share putting out the rubbish, cleaning the loo, changing the bed sheets and supervising any workmen who come to the house. For couples with children I am sure the agreement would be different.

In 1970 the American feminist writer Alix Kates Shulman published 'A Marriage Agreement' in the feminist journal *Up From Under*. She had found that the distribution of labour pre-children seemed fine, but that after having children tasks were divided along traditional gender roles. Writing some years later about the agreement, she wrote:

The idea was simply this: that a woman and man should share equally the responsibility for their household and children in every way, from the insidiously unacknowledged tasks of daily life to the pleasures of guiding a young human to maturity.

The agreement listed tasks that needed doing and explained how she and her partner would split them, from the task of preparing breakfast to making the beds to arranging babysitters. Behind all this were several key principles including 'We reject the notion that the work which brings in more money is the more valuable' and 'As parents we believe we must share all responsibility for taking care of our children and home – not only the work but the responsibility.'

These principles translated into rules such as 'Babysitters must be called by whoever the sitter is to replace. If no sitter turns up, the parent whose night it is to take responsibility must stay home' and 'Weekends: Split equally. Husband is free all of Saturday, wife is free all of Sunday, except that the husband does all weekend transportation, breakfasts and special shopping [to make up for wife's care during working hours in week].'

In some respects this sounds pretty great to me other than that there seems little time to be together as a family with both parents present. However, relationships are not supposed to be a contract worked out like a business arrangement. Some weeks I do more, some weeks my partner does, and a kind of balance that works for us has happened organically. But Alix Kates Shulman's contract certainly seems better to me than this anecdote that makes my blood boil, that was told to me by a feminist writer as an example of how traditional gender roles can work for some people.

She told me of a man and a woman who took on traditional roles, the man going to work and the woman looking after the home. One day, out of the home, someone asked him whether he would like some macaroni cheese. 'No thank you,' he said 'I don't like macaroni cheese.' His wife was astounded. She had been making him macaroni cheese, and he had been eating it, once a week for the duration of their long marriage. 'Why didn't you tell me?' she asked. 'Well,' her husband replied, 'I wouldn't want you to tell me how to do my job and I wouldn't presume to tell you how to do yours.'

To me, this isn't an example of traditional gender roles working well. First, why should the man have to eat something he doesn't like week in week out? And second, putting aside how this particular couple divides labour, what kind of partnership is it where the partners do not discuss their days and their likes and dislikes and take advice from each other. My marriage agreement may not be as prescriptive as Alix Kates Shulman's, but it would certainly include a period of time for talking honestly and openly.

Whose fault is adultery?

A weekend supplement recently included this fact in their relationship pages, alone in a box as a 'look at this – the world has gone crazy' kind of fact:

> *Did you know that recent research among divorce lawyers has found that in forty-five per cent of cases where infidelity is cited, women are the guilty party?*

Well here's a fact for you. Did you know that recent research among divorce lawyers has found that in fifty-five per cent of cases where infidelity is cited, men are the guilty party?

You only get hit thirty-five times

What would you do if your partner hit you? It's easy to say, when not in this situation, that you would leave any such partner immediately. Or to say that once may be because you provoked him, or because he saw red, or because he didn't know what he was capable of doing and is truly shocked at himself, and that you'll forgive once but not twice so if it ever happens again then you'll definitely leave him.

It may be easy to say that, but we know for most women, leaving is not as easy as that. We know that women with abusive partners do not tend to leave them after being hit once or even after being hit twice. No, on average a victim is assaulted thirty-five times before contacting the police, and many more never report it at all – other research (by Victim Support) suggests that as little as two per cent of domestic violence is reported.

Of course it is easy to be angered by this and to assume you would report your suspicions, if you had any, or help a friend leave an abusive partner. But what do you do when you are confronted with it for real? A friend of mine suffered low-level domestic violence for some time – an aggressive partner who would, during arguments, throw things at her. Did I help her? I am not sure that I did. She could have come to stay with me, of course, but I live nowhere near where she had made her life and had a job. Did I call the police? No, she would have hated me for that. Did I encourage her to leave the relationship? Of course, but when finances are intertwined and there are children involved, this isn't as easy as it sounds.

So what can we do to help end violence towards women? In part we need a high profile campaign that lets people know that domestic violence is unacceptable. A model for this might be the NSPCC's Full Stop campaign which has not asked for specific actions from supporters but has done very well at getting across the message that child abuse is not welcome in our society.

We also need to address the root of the problem of course – the perpetrators of violence. One domestic violence campaigner said to me that their advice to prevent domestic violence would be to never live with a heterosexual man. This does an injustice to most men of course, but does somewhat illustrate the scale of the problem. More practical is to ensure violence against women is not glamorised by the media and to teach men while still at school that such behaviour will not be tolerated.

And it is vitally important that women have the skills needed to look after themselves if they decide to leave their partner. This includes knowing how to access money and how to deal with bureaucracy. As Claire Kober, a campaigner who works for

Family Action (previously the Family Welfare Association) which helps families with a range of challenges, told me:

> *Too much of the domestic violence sector focuses on emergency steps such as the provision of refuges at the expense of the basic things such as what happens if you've been denied a bank account, never been in control of your money, have been forced to give up work and denied a career (preventing women from being or becoming financially independent) or have been saddled with debts by your partner meaning that even if you do manage to leave you're left with debts preventing you from re-establishing yourself.*

What Kober is in favour of is 'economic empowerment' classes that teach women how to handle these things. If these were offered as a matter of course to young women then women wouldn't be stuck in abusive relationships through fear of not being able to cope if they were out of them, and leaving such a relationship or marriage would really be an option.

Single women are feminists too

In some ways the author Helen Fielding's invention of Bridget Jones was great. Here was a character who helped the older generation understand the life of noughtie women – the importance of friends, the worries about being single for ever, the wine drinking and calorie counting. But in other ways, she created a new stereotype with which to beat women – that of the mid thirties single woman desperate for a man.

I suppose this stereotype is better than the previous one, that of a spinster. In her excellent book *Singled Out*, Virginia Nicholson looks at the period in the 1920s and 1930s when there were 1.75 million more women than men (partly due to the huge casualties of the First World War and partly due to immigration to the new world). There just weren't enough men to go round and the 'surplus' women had to adjust to life without the marriage they had always expected to have. For some of these women this was the making of them. Freed from the expectation of settling down some went on to have fascinating and high achieving careers of their own, something that would have been impossible for married women at the time. But many more were in low paid, low status positions, constantly worried for their own security, finding it difficult to make ends meet and tarred with the spinster brush. Interestingly men in China are soon to find themselves in the same position due to the one child policy and the preference for male children. It will be interesting to see what happens there.

A friend of mine, mid thirties and single, asked me what relevance feminism has to her. After all she doesn't have to worry about who does the housework as she is the only person in her household. Nor does she have to think about who looks after the children as she has none, or who pays the bills. That she should have solidarity with other women who do have to face those questions didn't wash. For my friend, the bond of just being a woman wasn't enough.

But feminism is incredibly relevant to her. As with all women, single or not, she has the right to walk down the street without fear of attack. She also has workplace issues regarding pay and promotion. She has decisions to make about dating and sex and contraception. And she too must decide whether to wear make-up, what to do about her body hair and what clothes to wear. But more than that, if she is not filling the roles historically regarded as women's most important roles – wife and mother – then feminism for her should be about ensuring she is not seen as a lesser person for this, either by other women or by men.

9

Children

For some people children are our whole reason for being here, or if not the reason then certainly the answer to a fulfilling life. For others, children are something to be avoided, the easiest way to ruin a nice and ordered existence. But whatever choices you make, whether you choose to have children or not and at what point in your life you make this decision, there are feminist implications. These range from the division of labour at home once children arrive to your role in the workplace once you are a mother, from the way society views childless women to whether, if you do have children, you buy them clothes in pink or blue.

I faced a difficult decision over whether to include abortion in this section – certainly I have included contraception in the chapter on sex. But because of the language the abortion debate tends to be framed in, focusing on the foetus as a potential baby, I decided to include it in children. This does not mean, however, that I think a foetus has the same rights as a child.

And of course having children leads to myriad decisions to be made every day, each with their own social implications, from what food to feed them and who makes it to what clothes to dress them in and what activities to enrol them in. If the daughter of two feminists asks for pink clothes, dollies and ballet lessons while their son asks for toy cars and a catapult, what should the feminist parents do? On an even more serious note, what do you do when the welfare of the individual child may be at odds with your beliefs about society in general, for example over education where you may feel a girls' school is better for your daughter but you may disagree with single-sex education generally? None of these choices are easy, but all have to be made.

Pro-choice, whatever your choice is

It bothers me that much of the feminist movement thinks that you have to be pro-abortion in order to be a feminist. Abortion is a moral issue and everybody has to be able to make up their own mind on such an emotive subject. To insist on support for this, the most difficult of moral areas, not only makes feminism inaccessible to many people who cannot bring themselves to support abortion, but also undermines the importance of choice in feminism. After all, 'choice' includes the right to disagree with something. But just as I believe that women who are opposed to abortion should have the choice not to have one, I hope that women who are anti-abortion believe that other women should also have the chance to make the opposite choice.

Noughtie girls are lucky. We are from one of the first generations in Britain to grow up knowing that, should we be in the position of having to make the choice, we can choose to terminate a pregnancy. And though I have never had to make this choice, I have appreciated knowing it is there.

When I was four days old, I was taken to a party where, by all accounts, I was cooed over and made a fuss of as any tiny baby is. The party, in 1978, was to mark the first anniversary of the opening of the day care abortion service, where my mum worked as a counsellor – though she was on maternity leave at the time.

I suspect some people will find this rather shocking, both the nature of my first party, and also that the people who worked there were not baby-hating monsters. In fact, those who worked for this service were people who placed great emphasis on life, but who felt strongly that women should be assisted, if they chose, to have safe and legal abortions.

Abortion is not a pleasant option. It is, in the emotive language of the anti lobby, killing babies. But in many circumstances continuing with a pregnancy is also not a good option. That may be because the woman is not ready for a baby, perhaps because her contraception failed or she made a mistake and got carried away in the heat of the moment. Or perhaps she was forced into sex. Or perhaps she just didn't think about the consequences of getting pregnant until it was too late. Maybe she feels her family is already complete – nearly half of women who have abortions have at least one child already. Or perhaps she has never wanted children. Or maybe the timing is all wrong. Whatever her reason, society has to allow her to make her own choice, not least because backstreet abortions pre-legalisation showed that abortion doesn't disappear if it is not legal, it just goes underground, and dangerously so.

So while I am not pro-abortion I am very pro-choice. After all, if you choose not to have an abortion you are still making a choice. And that is why I will stand up and fight for women to have the choice when it comes to abortion, because the anti-abortion lobby often fails to value the life of the woman and seeks to judge her at the most difficult time in her life. It is no good to wait until you want an abortion to join the pro-choice lobby. We need a pro-choice voice from women, and men, including those who have never faced an unwanted pregnancy but who have grown up safe in the knowledge that should they ever be in a situation where they have to make this decision, the choice is there.

How important is sperm?

Do men have a role to play in deciding whether a woman has an abortion? This is a hugely hard subject. After all, when we do have babies we are very keen to point out they are the responsibility of the father as well as the mother, both financially and emotionally.

In 2001 a British man, Stephen Hone, took legal action to stop his ex-girlfriend from having an abortion. He wanted his ex-girlfriend to keep the baby, and his case rested on his assertion that the correct legal procedures for an abortion had not been followed. The court ruled that although the correct procedures must be followed, once this was done the abortion could take place and that by law a man has no parental rights until their baby is born. This means that if the mother wants an abortion and the father does not, he cannot force her to have the child.

We can think more about this subject by looking at the 2001 film *Legally Blonde*, which may at first seem like a low brow summer movie, charming but not hugely relevant to real life, but is in fact an interesting feminist film. In it, the lead character, Elle Woods, played by Reese Witherspoon, is not only stereotypically feminine, spending much of her time in beauty salons, but also highly intelligent. When her boyfriend finishes with her and heads to Harvard Law School, Elle pulls out all the stops to get on the same course, and to win him back from his old school sweetheart. In one scene there is a law lecture going on with a sample case in which a man, a habitual sperm donor, has been harassing the parents of his biological child for visitation rights and is accused of stalking. Elle's ex-boyfriend makes the point that without this man's sperm the child would not exist. It looks like the ex may be winning his argument. Merely by virtue of providing the sperm, the man should have some rights over the child, he argues. But then Elle steps in. 'I have to wonder if the defendant kept a thorough record of each sperm emission made throughout his life?' she asks. The class laughs but she continues: 'Well, unless the defendant attempted to contact every single one-night-stand to determine if a child resulted in those unions then he has no parental claim whatsoever over this child. Why this sperm? Why now? For that matter, all masturbatory emissions where his sperm was clearly not seeking an egg could be termed reckless abandonment.'

This is clearly nonsense. Sperm not seeking an egg is no more abandonment than a woman failing to try to conceive every single cycle. But it illustrates rather well the futility of trying to claim rights over something that is not yet a baby. But ultimately what the argument must come down to, if we are to avoid stalemate in situations where the man and woman want different things, is that it is the woman who carries the child through pregnancy and the woman who gives birth. Realistically it is also the woman who is going to take on the majority of the caring role for that child. Therefore, should men have a say in whether an abortion can take place? The call, though a tough one, is no.

Trust us to know our own mind

It is not wholly true that there is unfettered access to abortion in the UK. To start with, in Northern Ireland where almost 1.8 million people live, there is no abortion at all. (One lawyer once told me that if the Unionists wanted to ensure Northern Ireland never becomes part of the Republic of Ireland they just have to legalise abortion, but they won't do it.)

In England, Scotland and Wales where a woman has access to abortion before twenty-four weeks of pregnancy, she must, legally at least, fit into one of four categories. These are that having the baby would harm her mental or physical health more than having the abortion, that having the baby would harm the mental or physical health of any children she already has, that the abortion is necessary to save the woman's life or prevent serious permanent harm to her mental or physical health or finally, that there is a high risk that the baby would be seriously handicapped.

Essentially, what this means is that women cannot just say they don't want a baby, they have to convince medical professionals that they fit into one of these categories. What is more, women can't just convince one doctor that this is the case, they have to convince two doctors before they are allowed an abortion, and any doctor is allowed to refuse this for their own moral reasons, though they have to then refer the woman to another doctor.

This is a farce because, as with emergency contraception, women just learn to play the system and know what to say in order to get what they need. This may work in terms of getting the abortion, but it does force women to lie, something that shouldn't be necessary. Deciding to have an abortion is traumatic enough without having to lie about it to medical professionals.

What we need is to abolish the two-doctor rule and take moral judgements away from doctors, and have an on demand abortion service. Women know abortion is not a nice option, but they are also responsible enough to be able to decide for themselves whether they want one.

Nine months of terror

As if pregnancy isn't a scary enough time anyway, the papers seem to go out of their way to make it even scarier. Read a daily paper regularly for the nine months of your pregnancy and you will be terrified.

Supposing you had conceived in August 2006 with a due date of April 2007. Not only would you have had the normal worries about the development of your baby and the impending labour, plus fears from regular coverage about the lack of midwives and the conditions of local maternity services, but you may have read articles telling you that eating fast food damages the thyroid gland in babies, that aspirin leads to heart defects and that even the scan can lead to brain abnormalities. Not enough vitamin E leads to your baby having asthma though apples may decrease the risk, and not enough vitamin D will give it weak bones. Smoking while pregnant will lead to hyperactive children, but some gases found in cigarette smoke can help prevent pre-eclampsia. Being too fat may have some health risks, but being too skinny can lead to miscarriage. And getting stressed by all this information? Well that will do no good at all – it could lead to your baby having problems with social skills, language ability and memory. And for the mother with just the right amount of apples and vitamin D, who never takes an aspirin, who never eats fast food, who is neither too fat nor too thin. Well that's irrelevant if she lives in Oxford, Lewisham, North Lincolnshire, Rotherham, Kingston upon Hull, Haringey, Hastings, North East Lincolnshire, Waltham Forest or Reading – her baby will still have a tough time according to news reports that they are the worst places in Britain to bring up children.

I'll tell you what would help women. Sensible advice, better post birth support, a culture where misinformation is nipped in the bud and an end to all the scare stories that make women feel they are doing the wrong thing whatever they do.

The same old problem

Nearly forty years after Alix Kates Shulman wrote her marriage contract (see chapter 8), the Family and Parenting Institute's report *Listening to Mother: Making Britain Mother Friendly* by Sally Gimson found the same problems still exist for women having children:

> *It used to be that marriage was the turning point for women, but that is no longer the case. Women get married or cohabit and their lives remain remarkably similar. They continue in their full-time jobs and some keep their own name. The level of commitment to the person they marry or live with may alter substantially, but there are few other outside pressures on the relationship … It is no wonder that women are lulled into a false sense of security, believing that having children will have little effect on their lives.*

The idea of a woman who has it all is one of the great successes of feminism. Thanks to the work of the feminists who went before us, it is no longer odd for a woman to have both a career and a family. In fact this is not just possible, but expected, by others and by the women themselves. We are supposed to be superwomen who can juggle all aspects of our lives.

This has a huge impact on family life however. Women end up doing their job and the bulk of the domestic labour and childcare while men, clawing their way up the career ladder while their partners have children, work longer hours than ever, forty-eight hours a week for more than a third of working fathers. They also want to have it all but work patterns mean time off to spend with their children is sparse.

In Britain, government policy in the noughties has been for mothers to go back to work after their children are very young. This is seen as particularly good for poorer women, a way to be part of society rather than on its edge. But, says the Family and Parenting Institute, this has not made women equal to men. Instead it has meant most women struggle on caring for children and working, often in badly paid work.

In 1987 Valerie Grove started writing a book called *The Compleat Woman: Marriage, Motherhood, Career – Can She Have it All?* in which she looked at women who supposedly have it all – successful marriages lasting over twenty-five years, large families of three or more children and a successful career.

Viv Groskop revisited the idea of the 'compleat woman' in an article for the *Guardian* in 2008 to see whether such women still exist and found that if such a life was hard twenty years ago then it is practically impossible these days, with two full time incomes needed to support a modern lifestyle, high divorce rates and low birth rates.

Of course not having these three things does not make a woman less valid, as Grove was keen to point out to Groskop, telling her that she 'wasn't intending to imply that anyone who didn't have these things was incomplete'. Nevertheless, says Groskop, these attributes – the marriage, the children and the career – are what many young women today would like and what few will get.

It is certainly what I would like in an ideal world but I also accept that it may not be possible – if I want to spend time with my future children, perhaps my career will suffer. I may want a long marriage, but statistically I have to accept that it may not happen. The beauty of noughtie girl feminism of course is that I can say this is what I want without feeling any less of a feminist for having children and marriage as part of my aspiration, even, dare I say it, as more important to me than the career part. But I should remember as I try to achieve this, the warnings of the Family and Parenting Institute, that the aspirations I have to have it all, which are shared by many other noughtie girls, will only be possible if we continue to push for support in the workplace and support at home.

Can my daughters wear pink (and can my sons play with guns)?

A friend of mine spent the last week of her pregnancy writing annoyed letters to children's shops about their lack of any baby clothes that were not pink, blue or an insipid shade of yellow.

When shops replied it was to tell her that their market research had shown that was what mothers wanted. It was not, she replied, what this particular mother wanted. Nevertheless, forced through lack of alternatives, many women have no choice but to predominantly use pink for a girl and blue for a boy.

The socialisation of children doesn't just happen in the home. Even if they live in a house where the cooking, cleaning and shopping are done equally by their mother and their father, even if both parents share the driving, empty the bins, invite people for dinner and watch the same television programmes, outside of the home they will be bombarded with influences about how men and women are supposed to act.

This may explain the anecdote from a friend of mine who insists that it is irrelevant whether you buy your daughters toys specifically for girls and your sons toys specifically for boys: 'My sister bought both her boy and her girl a toy buggy – my niece used it to ferry her dollies round and my nephew used it to ram raid anything he came across.'

The trouble is not with an individual girl wishing to pretend she is keeping house or enjoying pink and glitter, or with an individual boy preferring 'masculine' colours or boisterous play. It is with the expectation of this and the way it is viewed as the norm or as the only way for that child to fit in, and the way in which there is no choice for parents (or children). Polly Toynbee wrote about this 'girlification' of clothes and toys:

> It's almost impossible to buy toys now that are not putridly pink branded or aggressively superhero male. Bikes, sleeping bags, lunch boxes, nothing is neutral now, everything Barbie and Bratz. Princess tiaras, fairy and ballerina dressing up, pink, pink everywhere – and it damages girls' brains. That's before you start on thongs for seven-year-olds and sexy slogans on three-year-olds' T-shirts – girlification.

Of course there is nothing intrinsically wrong with pink. I am a grown woman and I like it. Many women do and that is why the breast cancer awareness campaign uses pink with such success from pink ribbons to pink underwear and even pink scrabble sets.

But that there is no escaping from girlification should worry us, in case the lack of choice in clothing and toys for our daughters is soon reflected in a lack of choice elsewhere in their lives.

Stay at home dads

What if you have children and you want to be the main caregiver, but you have competition in this from the child's father? I don't have children but I have spent rather a long time looking forward to the day when I do, and in my mind when that day comes although I want their father to be very much involved, I see myself as the main carer while my partner works full time. This is not because of a notion about what is women's work, or as an anti-feminist thing, but because that's what I want to do. It's what most women either want to do, or are forced into for financial or social reasons.

Of course I can understand why men might want a piece of this for themselves, wanting to be at home to get the joy of bringing someone up, seeing children discover new things and generally being a parent. But do I feel threatened by the idea that men might usurp women in automatically assuming a right to this role? I'm afraid I do. I suspect that this is how men in the boardroom feel about women in the workplace, which doesn't mean either of us is right, but does perhaps make it more understandable. This once again reminds us that while feminism is about equality and about choice, not all of the fruits of equality will necessarily be welcomed by us all, and while I believe we need it, I think it's important to recognise that when feminism is realised and equality comes, there may be things we don't like about equality as well as things that we do.

Natural born carers

Having said that, I don't claim that looking after children is easy or even fun a lot of the time. It is a role full of drudgery, from changing nappies, washing clothes and sterilising equipment to the constant attention babies and children need.

Men know this – do it for a day or two and they expect plaudits as a superdad whereas women who look after children day in and day out are rarely supermum – no that title is reserved for women who do this and have a spectacular job.

As I said above, when the time comes I think this is a role I want. That may annoy some feminists, but that is how I feel. What I don't feel is that women are naturally born to the role and that men are not, a misogynistic excuse for men not doing enough of the parenting. Take this article by James Delingpole in the *Telegraph* in 2008 headlined 'Men Are Made To Work Not Rear Children', in which the author makes excuses for not attending his children's school events and talks about his role as the provider for his family. But here's what sickened me most of all, his explanation that as a man he just isn't cut out for childcare:

> *We're great at the fun, irresponsible stuff: swinging our kids till their arms almost come out of their sockets; jokily throwing balls at them, making them cry and getting told off by our wives; letting them stand up on the wall of the lion enclosure. That is because we instinctively know that our task is to nurture our offsprings' sense of risk and adventure. And also because we're basically still children ourselves. What we can't do, and never will be able to, is cope with the sheer attrition and grind of child-rearing in that brilliant, professional way our womenfolk can. We can't multi-task; we're too easily distracted; we're basically a bit rubbish. And this isn't an excuse. This is a fact.*

Does he really think that women are born knowing how to change a nappy? What narrow-minded rubbish. The same goes for the wife of a celebrity that I saw interviewed on television explaining why her husband wasn't at the birth of their children – he's not very good at doctors, hospitals and schools, that kind of thing, she said. Fine, some people are not very good at hospitals. But it struck me that this was actually just an excuse for a man who didn't want to be fully involved, like Delingpole. Because women may not like the blood and bodily fluids of the maternity ward either, or the drudgery of everyday life at home with kids, but they don't usually have a choice. What Delingpole wrote and what the hospital phobic celebrity said are just excuses for not being fully involved in parenting, and should be unacceptable.

In order to avoid this kind of excuse, as a society we also need to make changes and to involve dads more with their children. For example, a friend of mine with two children at secondary school had an ongoing battle with his school to be kept informed of parent evenings and school plays, despite government guidelines that say both parents have the same right to participate in decisions about a child's education and receive information about the child. Despite speaking to the head of the school about this several times, getting information on his children's progress and invites to parent evenings proved an uphill struggle. A less tenacious man may have given up.

Similarly we make it difficult for men to be involved with their children in public, from simple things like a lack of baby changing facilities available to men (many are in the women's toilets) to a general sense that men with young children are a little bit suspicious.

What we need to do as noughties feminists is make a society in which men are encouraged and expected to be fully involved with every aspect of their children's lives. But within this each partnership has to be allowed to be different – modern day noughties feminism has to be about women being able to feel comfortable saying that they do want to have a caring role as much as being about being able to say they don't want to have it. Neither of these though should be seized by men and used as an excuse for not being naturally good at parenting and if they do, well more fool us if we let them get away with it.

From here to maternity

There have been a lot of headlines in the noughties about the employability of women of childbearing age, especially as changes to maternity leave have given women the right to up to a year off work with much of it paid. At least two high profile male businessmen have said they avoid hiring women of child-bearing age for this reason, and some high profile women have said the same.

Not only do these attitudes discriminate against women who want or have children, but also against those who don't. Given that 'child-bearing age' is from early teens to late forties, this is an awfully long time for women to be unemployable and has a huge impact on equality and also, of course, the economy. But the thing is, the way the law currently stands with there being far more maternity provision than paternity provision, I do understand why businesses, particularly small businesses, feel like this.

There is only one way to stop this specific form of discrimination against women in the workplace, and that is to make parental leave something that men and women get in equal amounts, so that the loss to the employer is the same whether they employ a man or a woman.

At the moment fathers are only entitled to two weeks of paternity leave, and this is paid at a very low statutory rate. In many cases families cannot afford for men to take this. Mothers get more than this, though still not enough to be classed as generous – six weeks of leave with ninety per cent of their normal pay packet and a weekly allowance for a further thirty-three weeks, unless their employer offers a better package than they are compelled to.

We need a flexible parental leave policy which can be taken by either men or women thus ending the discrimination in job interviews that assumes women will take time out of work to have children. If men are as likely to take time out as women this discrimination is pointless for employers. This is what happens in Norway where not only do fathers get six weeks of paid parental leave but parents have the right to choose how the rest of their parental leave is divided between them. Similarly men and women should both have the right to work flexibly after they have children unless there is a very good reason why not.

But we need more than that. With such low rates of statutory maternity and paternity pay after the first few weeks we are in a position where extended parental leave is only possible for richer families. If the government wants a more equal society and one in which all families can afford to spend time with their very young children, they need to subsidise better maternity and paternity pay packages and to support businesses to be able to offer this.

We also need to make it impossible for people to discriminate against women for being women. Perhaps we need to learn a lesson from orchestras where it is common practice for auditions to be conducted behind a screen, so that the panel cannot see whether candidates are male or female and can instead focus on their playing.

But we also need to change our expectations and culture so that it is the norm for men to take time off when they become fathers so that when men fail to do this people ask why. If we remove the financial barriers to men playing a full parenting role, then we can start to focus on the social barriers that stop men being fully involved. Because it may be a cliché but it is a true cliché, that no man is going to get to his deathbed and look back on his life and wish he'd spent more time at the office, but he will look back at his children and wish he'd spent more time with them.

Educating your girls

Thankfully the time has gone when people educated their boys but not their girls and when education for girls was predominantly about learning domestic tasks. Nevertheless there are still questions to be asked and souls to be searched when it comes to educating your girls.

You may think that sending girls to a girls' school is the most feminist option, so that girls can learn without being intimidated by boys. You may think that paying for the best education possible is the way forward so your girls have the most opportunities in life. You may believe in single sex education for girls but mixed schools for boys, like people who send their girls to a single sex school and their boys to mixed schools to benefit at the expense of other people's girls. You may, as some parents do, send your daughters to a less good school than your sons on the basis that you don't think she would cope in the rough and tumble of a sporty co-educational environment whereas your sons would flourish. Make whatever excuses you want to in order to justify the decisions you make about your own child but I must tell you – all of this is anti-feminist.

If we are to create a society in which girls and boys have a true equality of opportunity then we have to start this from the earliest age possible. You may have a shy daughter who feels more comfortable in a girls' school and is happier in that environment to answer questions in class or take part in sport. You may have a son easily distracted by having girls present, inclined to show off or take work less seriously. That may be, but the feminist way is to deal with this and find solutions to the problem rather than put the problem on hold until later in life.

I know that every parent wants what they think is best for their child. But really, we do better by our daughters by giving them the confidence to do the best they can in mixed sex environments, because life isn't single sex, and sooner or later they are going to have to deal with that.

10

Forward feminism

In some senses, Western women are very lucky. We aren't, on the whole, honour killed. Our genitals are not mutilated as they are in countries that practise female circumcision. We can own property. We can vote. We can afford sanitary towels or tampons.

As the social anthropologist Alan Macfarlane puts it in his book *Letters to Lily*, the Western woman has never had it so good:

> You have education, lovely clothes, good food, doctors, dentists and hospitals freely available, loving parents, political and religious freedom. You do not have to slave with your body and you can choose what you want to do in your life, when and whom you will marry, whether to have children. You believe you are equal to any man and that you will live to a ripe

old age, benefiting from a pension in a country where there are no secret police and no extortionate landlords to live off you. Above all, you live in peace and free from serious violence and fear.

He is right. We are lucky. The feminists of previous generations won huge battles for us. Nowadays it is hard to believe that it wasn't until the mid seventies that women could get a mortgage without needing a male signatory. Or the mid sixties that women could wear trousers to work at the BBC. But in some ways these great leaps forward for feminism have made our position as noughtie girls difficult because we look ungrateful when we ask for more. But as I wrote in the introduction to this book, feminism for women today is not about wanting to be better off than we were, it's about wanting equality. Where the fight is almost won, the battles are more difficult, because it looks as if we are being greedy.

Take these examples from my life recently:

- I received a letter meant for me but addressed to me using the wrong title (Mrs) and my husband's initial and surname.
- I got the bus home late at night and had to look behind me several times as I walked to my house to check that I was safe.
- I read a glossy magazine aimed at women in their 30s and there wasn't a single woman above a size 12 pictured, except in a story about an obese woman.

- I tried to buy presents for the newborn babies of my friends, and found it very hard to find anything not in pink or blue.
- At an expensive restaurant my husband and I ate in only one menu had prices on it, and it was given to him, as was the bill.
- I had lunch with four friends, three of whom have babies, all of whom were looking after them while their male partners were at work.
- A male friend's grandmother cooked us breakfast and, without asking what we wanted, gave me one egg and my friend two.
- I noticed the toilet was filthy and didn't clean it. Nobody else did either.

Each of these may look like a small issue. And they are small in comparison to winning the vote or getting equal pay. But once again, we are not fighting to be more equal, we are fighting to be equal. If we don't sweat the small stuff then we accept that inequality is acceptable.

The journalist Madeleine Bunting sums up this situation well:

How do you measure the progress of a revolutionary movement like feminism? Do you judge the highest number of women in parliament ever as a significant milestone, or still woefully short of fully representing the female proportion of the population? Is it a sign of failure that our daughters will still have battles to fight in twenty years, or can we seize upon the fact that women make

up more than half the university intake? Do you look back to
see how far women's lives have changed in the last generation,
or look around you at the struggles which still dominate many
women's lives? Are you the kind of person who looks at a glass
half empty, or half full?

How you interpret this progress, and whether you are a half empty or half full person is an issue for every noughtie girl to grapple with. But once you've decided that feminism isn't the ogre it's been made out to be, once you've accepted that feminism is about being free to make your own choices and being given true equality, once you've recognised that feminism is a broad church encompassing all skirt lengths and haircuts, what can you actually do to take things forward?

Women in politics

At the time of writing this we have 125 women MPs in the House of Commons. That might seem like a lot, in fact it is a lot considering how few there were not so long ago, but it is out of a total of 645 and therefore hardly any at all given that women make up half of the population.

Sometimes the debate around this focuses on the need for more women MPs in order for women's issues to be taken more seriously. This bothers me hugely because there isn't really any such thing as a 'women's issue'. Yes, a woman may be more naturally tuned into the needs of women around childcare, other caring roles or domestic violence, because she may have direct experience of these things, but why would she not also be interested in traditionally male areas such as business, transport and foreign affairs? After all, if you asked 'How would a politician or political party appeal to a man?' the answer would be 'It depends what the man is interested in.' The same goes for women.

When political parties talk about women as a group what they really seem to be doing is talking about mothers, using women's issues as a political euphemism for childcare and education. This is a mistake because it alienates other groups of women. A 2005 Age Concern and Fawcett Society report looked at women fifty-five and over and found their concerns were far from the concerns of women twenty years younger. Their main concerns were, in order, the NHS, pensions, public services and the economy.

If politicians insist on treating women as a homogenous group, no wonder many women are turned off politics, thinking it isn't for them. And if that doesn't turn women off politics, the language should. For women are often spoken about in terms of 'wooing' or 'courting' women voters, as if we are there to be won. It's a mistake of course, if politicians want a lasting relationship with us. For flirting, as we all know, may spark initial interest. It may even lead to us getting into bed with the flirter for a while. But, if a relationship is to last when the initial attraction is over, we want promises to be kept and to share with our partner moral values and dreams for the future.

It's not just the language and the grouping us together that is the problem though. The Fawcett Society, an organisation which campaigns for equal rights for women, blames what it calls 'the four C's' for stopping more women getting involved in politics. They are culture, childcare, cash and confidence. That is, the confrontational culture of British politics, the childcare and other caring responsibilities that mean they do not have time for politics, the cash it costs to visit areas where you would like to stand for election and to produce campaign materials and the lack of confidence needed to put yourself forward and face multiple selection committees.

I agree with the second, third and fourth C, but the first C is rather patronising. Saying that women don't like confrontation, can't handle the debating nature of the House of Commons and would, if we ruled the world, all sit together around a scented candle makes me want to take the said candle and shove it up the arse of whoever said this. Nothing makes me want to take a machine gun and blast away indiscriminately more than when I hear people say that if women ruled the world there would be no more wars.

I don't want to fall into the trap of saying that only women can represent women. This is clearly not true. After all, having Margaret Thatcher as Prime Minister from 1979–1990 may have helped little girls think they could grow up to do anything they wanted, but it did not further the cause of women in their everyday lives. No, women can be represented by men just as women could also do a good job of representing men.

In fact, in her book *The New Feminism*, Natasha Walter tackled the issue of whether Thatcher can be a feminist icon despite having done so little for women in terms of actual policies.

> *Women who complain that Margaret Thatcher was not a feminist because she didn't help other women or openly acknowledge her debt to feminism have a point but they are also missing something vital. She normalised female success. She showed that although feminine power and masculine power may have different languages, different metaphors, different appearances, different gestures, different traditions, different ways of being glamorous or nasty, they are equally strong, equally valid ... No one can ever question whether women are capable of single-minded vigour, or efficient leadership, after Margaret Thatcher. She is the great unsung heroine of British feminism.*

During much of my childhood Margaret Thatcher was Prime Minister. Her politics are not my politics and I recognise she did little policy wise for women. But I think Walter is right that the very fact there was a woman at the top has made women of my generation feel they have every right to be at the forefront of the power making structures of society. If we build on this and ensure women don't just make it to the top, but are equally represented at every level of politics, then our daughters will know no bounds.

Lock up your sons

Remember Michael Moore and his hit of the second year of the noughties, *Stupid White Men*? It was an invective against the people running America who were mainly, said Moore, right wing, stupid, white and male. I was reminded of it when in a call I put out to charities asking for their ideas on inequality, I got the following message from road safety charity Brake.

Dear Ellie,

Just an idea: As a road safety charity, we see that women born in the 1970s, 1980s and 1990s are some of the safest drivers on our roads. However, far too many of these women at some point in their lives, will be affected by road crashes, either directly or by losing someone they love and statistics show the majority of these crashes are caused by men.

Despite a long-standing debate about which gender make the better drivers, the majority of driving offences are caused by men. Ninety-four per cent of drivers found guilty of causing death by dangerous driving are male and ninety-seven per cent of drivers found guilty of dangerous driving are male. In the UK, forty per cent of male drivers could be classed as 'high violators', compared with twenty per cent of female drivers. Violations included such behaviours as speeding, crossing on a red light, driving too close to the vehicle in front or driving over the legal limit for blood alcohol.

Please let me know if this is of interest to you.

I love this email. What feminist wouldn't? It's a reminder of all the ills men cause in society wrapped up in some statistics from a reputable charity. In short, men cause accidents, women cope with the damage later.

But what are we to do about this? We could ban all men from driving I suppose, though women would just be pestered for lifts the whole time instead, plus it would be somewhat unfair to the men who do drive as safely as possible.

Brake's recommendations are less drastic. Their suggestions include more research into gender differences and how they typically affect attitudes towards road safety, awareness-raising publicity campaigns which specifically target male drivers and compulsory road safety education in schools.

But what if we banned men from driving and claimed it was for their own good? Given that men aged between eighteen and twenty-five are more likely to be attacked than anyone else in society, having a ban on being outside their own homes for men up to the age of twenty-five could kill two birds with one stone and prevent all of these attacks and all of these accidents.

I'm joking of course – you can't really put a curfew on men (though some countries do restrict women's movements in such a way), and we wouldn't really want to – but it reminded me of a funny anecdote from the journalist and campaigner Julie Bindel about the hunt for the Yorkshire Ripper, when police decided to advise women to stay indoors and to only leave the house if absolutely necessary and accompanied by a man.

My women's group mocked up police notices and fly posted them all over the city. 'Attention all men in West Yorkshire,' the notice read, 'there is a serial killer on the loose in the area. Out of consideration for the safety of women, please ensure you are indoors by 8pm each evening, so that women can go about their business without the fear you may provoke.'

What you can do – a (wo)manifesto for change

A school friend of mine told me she doesn't consider herself a feminist, not because she doesn't believe in the aims of the movement but because she doesn't feel worthy of the name:

The reason that I wouldn't use the term feminist is because I would describe it as a doing word and I have done nothing that would lead me to call myself a feminist. I lack the passion and dedication that these things involve. I have never gone on a march, or made my feelings known on gender inequality issues in any kind of official manner. If any of this is included in your book this would be the nearest I have come to letting my thoughts be known in an active manner.

I disagree with my friend on this. If feminism, as a word or as a movement, is to move away from being a term of abuse, then it has to be mainstream, a word used by more than just those making the loudest noise. You don't have to do anything to be a feminist, you just have to think you are one.

Another friend disagrees with me that it is important to make an issue over who washes the pants in her household. She says that if she was told that she had to wash her boyfriend's pants or there was a law saying that she had to then it would become as important to her as abortion rights, but to her the feminist fight is about determining priorities. She is right in a way because of course some issues are more important than others. But noughtie girl feminism has to be as much about being seen to be equal as being equal, so if you choose to campaign on getting more non-pink baby clothes into shops, or having as many men in adverts for washing up powder as you do women, or on more public toilets, then that is as valid and as important to the feminist campaign as abortion rights or equal pay.

So whatever your priorities, and whatever level you want your activism to take place on, here are some simple ideas for how you can be part of the noughtie girl feminist fight.

1. Define what you mean by feminist. You can't be a feminist if you don't know what you mean by that, so work out a sentence to explain yourself to people who challenge you, even if it is something simple like 'I am a feminist because I believe men and women should be equal.' And don't just define feminism, but be proud of it. For too long it's been something we're shifty about. I am not suggesting you have to wear badges or t-shirts with slogans if you don't want to. But when you're asked what you believe in say proudly that you are a feminist. If you are proud of this then others will be too.

2. Get involved in a campaign, however small. We can't all change the world but we can make small changes

199

to the world around us. So sign a petition, write an angry letter or just refuse to buy anything with an anti-woman slogan. And don't let men you don't know call you 'babe'.

3. Make statements that declare your feminism. I am a Ms not a Miss or a Mrs and when people address me wrongly I correct them. Ensure you fill out forms to reflect this. Keep your own surname. Don't leave the finances to men. Pay your way when you are taken out for dinner. Get out of your seat on the train if a man standing up looks tired and like he needs it more than you. Don't make the tea in a meeting if you are the only woman. There are hundreds of feminist statements the noughtie girl can make every single day.

4. Stop thinking of women as a minority society should cater for out of the goodness of its heart – we make up half the population and our needs must be serviced. So that means things like ensuring women feel comfortable breast feeding in public and are safe walking home at night as a right, not as a favour.

5. Make your employers be socially responsible by asking for an Equal Pay Audit. Currently only an obligation in the public sector, an Equal Pay Audit will check that staff are being paid equal money for equal jobs regardless of gender. Your company may think it's not sexist but they may find some surprises. And if they're not sexist that's great news – get them to shout about

their equality from the rooftops and be proud of their contribution to feminism.

6. Do sweat the small stuff when it comes to language. I wouldn't go as far as calling for words such as women to be spelled wimmin, as some feminists of previous generations have done, but particularly in workplace situations we need to insist on removing the assumption our language makes that people in charge are men. So when I chair a meeting or a committee I am not the chairman. Nor am I a chairwoman. No, I am the chair.

7. Remember, and remind people, that feminist is totally different to feminine. You can be both, or neither, or just one of these but don't let people see feminine and feminist as opposites. In fact challenge people by talking about your feminism while wearing pink.

8. Campaign for women to be recognised formally. I can't walk down Whitehall in London without stopping for a moment to admire the Women of WWII Memorial. There are many other statues on Whitehall. They include statues of George Duke of Clarence, Lord Hartington the Eighth Duke of Devonshire, Earl Haig, James I and Walter Raleigh. That's right, not one of them is a woman. When there are public consultations on who to honour, suggest a woman, and when you see a glut of male statues, write to the relevant authority suggesting a statue gender audit.

9. Campaign for the UK as a whole to become more

feminist. We don't think about it much because the Queen had a son as her first born, Charles, and his first born was also a son, William. But men take priority over women when it comes to inheriting the throne. There are lots of other archaic and sexist rules in British Society. Did you know that unmarried daughters of members of the House of Lords have to sit in their own section if they want to watch proceedings, so that the unmarried sons can look at them to see who they wish to woo? And that invitations to some events hosted by members of the royal family will only be sent to a woman if she uses Miss or Mrs? Often sexist rules get forgiven for being 'tradition', a poor excuse for what is essentially a sexist system that discriminates against women.

10. One of the tools noughtie girls have at our disposal that previous generations of feminists didn't is the internet, a great democratising force because anyone can post anything online. Got something to say? Then blog or comment on other people's blogs. You don't need to wait for a male editor to accept your pitch, or a male television producer to make a programme for you. You can do it yourself and have access to millions of readers and viewers.

If it happened to men

If you ever start to doubt your feminism, have a think about what would happen if men were in the same position as women are today. For example, I wrote an article about the lack of access women in Zimbabwe have to sanitary products to use when they are on their period. Instead of using sanitary towels or tampons they are being forced to find alternate means of containing their menstrual blood, often having to use old newspaper or cloth, leading in many cases to infection.

I had trouble interesting most editors in running an article on this because periods were considered too icky for their readers. In the article I did finally get published I moaned about this. Is it because periods are just something that happen to women that this issue is being ignored I asked. If it were the other way round – if say penises were falling off, would the world take note?

This question applies to most issues of contemporary feminism. If men were earning less money than women for the same work, or having enforced career breaks and re-entering the jobs market at a lower level than when they left, wouldn't the world sit up and take notice? If men were unable to get home at night for fear of attack I bet there would suddenly be more street lighting and conductors on transport. If men were pregnant for nine months and had to deliver their babies and then take on the bulk of the caring role I bet there would be better paternity leave. And if men produced milk for babies I bet there would be no furtive tutting when they got their teats out in public.

Lessons in feminism
The feminist journalist Joan Smith write an article for *The Times*

in 2008 lamenting the lack of knowledge about feminism in young women these days and the lack of interest in women's studies courses and consciousness raising classes. Instead, she suggests, the subject should be tackled in schools, with classes on feminism for students. This is a great idea, but what would such lessons teach?

Well, they would need to be about more than the fact that the first Briton in space was a woman, Helen Sharman, or that Waterloo Bridge was mainly constructed by women, though facts like these are important too.

Perhaps the first subject pupils need to be taught about when it comes to feminism is how this country's system of government works. They have to know how to vote, how to stand for election, how to campaign, how to contact elected representatives and how to change things.

Confidence would be a huge part of any feminism classes too. Confidence to say yes, confidence to say no, confidence to try to achieve your best and not care what other people say. Classes would teach leadership too, and how to be led. Chairing meetings, accounts and letter writing would all come into it. So would body language and being able to use your voice assertively.

None of this is just feminism of course, or just for girls. These are skills that people need to be effective members of society generally. In fact nothing would help feminism more than a good knowledge of basic skills to ensure women are well equipped to enter the workplace and succeed in it.

We need better sex education too, not just to know how to avoid pregnancy but also how to get pregnant – it is amazing how many women do not know when ovulation occurs or the best ways to maximise chances of conception.

Feminism classes would be for boys too. As well as all of the above they need to know how to cook and that cooking is not just for women. Classes in childcare for both genders would also be helpful and perhaps some classes in how to clean, how to plan a menu and how to write a shopping list.

But feminism classes, even if they included all of this, amount to nothing if feminism is shunted into just one class rather than incorporated into the whole curriculum. At the moment if you are asked to picture a philosopher you probably think of a man in robes. Picture a scientist and you think of a man in a white coat. Picture an artist and you think of a man in a beret. Picture a mathematician and you think of a man scratching his head and looking at graph paper.

A feminist curriculum would ensure that history classes talk about women's role in history, as leaders and as part of the mass population. Science lessons would talk about women scientists as much as men. Economics needs to look at women's role in the economy and the implications of policies on women. Religious education has to look at where religion mistreats women and highlight this. In literature books by women must be read and discussed and books with strong female characters have to be studied. In art and music there must be discussions about why there are so few female composers and artists from history that we have heard of and those that we do know of must be studied.

Feminism classes could do worse than require every pupil to read and think about the book of poems by Carol Ann Duffy called *The World's Wife* in which she makes readers think about the women behind the men we have heard of. She takes the phrase 'behind every successful man is a great woman' (or 'surprised woman' or 'exhausted woman' depending which version of the quotation you choose, or even the Groucho Marx version 'behind every great man is a woman, and behind her is his wife') and gives us the story of the wives of famous men. Here's my favourite, granting Charles Darwin's wife the observation that changed the face of biology:

Mrs Darwin
7 April 1852

Went to the zoo.
I said to Him –
Something about that chimpanzee over there reminds me of you.

But even that is not enough. If feminism is to be taught in schools it should not just be in the content of lessons but in the whole ethos of the school, in which girls and boys must be equal in terms of both expectation and achievement. For feminism is too important to be a niche subject taught in just one classroom. It has to infiltrate every part of schools so that it cannot be identified as feminism but as a normal part of life.

A women's history month

Perhaps what we need, as well as feminism classes, is a women's history month. This doesn't mean the other eleven months of the year should be about men of course, but it would allow us a time to specifically focus on women's achievements. For although I started this book by saying that it doesn't matter whether noughtie girls know their place in feminist history as what matters is whether we are equal now, not whether we are closer to equality than in the past, I didn't mean that people shouldn't be aware of women in history, but rather that you don't need an intimate knowledge of academic feminism to be able to demand your rights.

We're not all going to go away and read the works of the many feminists who have gone before us, whether first wave, second wave, third wave or from some other wave, but we must acknowledge the role other feminists have played in shaping our world. Because of them we can vote, work, wear trousers, stand for parliament, in fact, do whatever we want. Therefore it is important to have something of a sense of how far women have come over history and how recent the gains in our freedom have been, if only to appreciate that our rights are fragile and we mustn't let our guard down as feminists or we might lose them.

What we need is an awareness month along the lines of Black History Month which takes place in the UK each October.

Schools could be encouraged to have displays and lessons on the history of women's rights. Art galleries could embrace women artists of the past in their exhibitions. Orchestras could play music by female composers. There could be consciousness raising campaigns about the plight of women around the world.

What mustn't happen though is to create such a month and then turn it into the kind of fluffy event in which women are presumed to only care about scented candles, in which women are assumed to avoid conflict at all costs, and where women are seen as being primarily interested in making cakes, especially wholesome ones made out of vegetables and brown flour.

Zoe Williams wrote an excellent article for the *Guardian* in May 2007 in which she railed against some of the types of activity that women's day events inspire:

> *Let's start by running through how different organisations have chosen to mark tomorrow's International Women's Day 2007. The Greater London Authority had an event last weekend with bike workshops, self-defence classes, some kind of spice-centric cookery display, and a fashion show by Kulture2Couture ... Meanwhile, in a talk entitled Animals in Art, 'successful female artist Sally Matthews' discusses the role of animals in art ... And the Ayr Bonnie Lassies promise a 'fun-filled day of dancing from around the world, yoga, storytelling and IT'.*

As Williams says, 'I want to take the piss, but I don't know where to start.'

But done properly, avoiding the yoga and the joss sticks and the carrot cake and focusing on human rights and suffrage and history, this could be a consciousness raising event for the whole of society, ensuring that women's rights are always on the agenda and to help remind everyone of past inequalities and future opportunities.

Pick 'n' mix feminism

Catherine Redfern of the feminist website *The F Word* wrote an article in which she talks about pick 'n' mix feminism where you take the parts of feminism you fancy from each thinker or movement. This pick 'n' mix idea is ideal for noughtie girls. We choose the bits of feminism we feel comfortable with and reject other bits. With pick 'n' mix sweets you have a bit of everything you fancy (or, if you are me, too much of everything you fancy) and leave the things you don't like out of your selection. With pick 'n' mix feminism it is the same. You can for example object to discrimination at work but be happy to take your husband's name. You might be anti-abortion but very keen to see a rise in female MPs.

One of the problems with feminism of previous generations is that there seemed to be an insistence that women embrace every aspect of the movement in an all or nothing kind of way. But noughtie girl feminists reject this idea of being told what to think, whoever it is by. Yes, we judge people for doing things that we consider not to be feminist, and we should be able to do so because being annoyed and making judgements is a key step in deciding to campaign for change. But as Jennifer Foote Sweeney wrote in an article for the American website www.salon.com, that doesn't mean we can judge whether or not someone else is a feminist if they themselves think they are:

> *I cling to the genteel idea that one does not grill one's sisters about their private lives in order to evaluate their commitment to the sisterhood. It has never been polite to ask someone about their salary or the colour of their pubic hair. Certainly it is not polite to ask a person why they got married or if they've had an abortion. And it is even more egregious if one is asking these questions to make sure that the victim's feminist papers are in order.*

Our pick 'n' mix feminism does not require an in depth knowledge of feminist theory. Open Germaine Greer's *The Female Eunuch* at random and you get a sentence like this:

> *If altruism is chimeric, it does not follow that all love behaviour is basically egotistical.*

This kind of language is immediately off-putting, not just because I don't have a clue what she is talking about but because the academic framework of this kind of book immediately seems removed from our everyday lives.

Instead noughtie girls define and understand their feminism by what we see around us every day, and from talking to our friends. For example, I know a woman who goes to pole dancing lessons. She does it for the exercise, and because it's fun. She even entered a competition and won a pole for her living room. Pole dancing of course is more normally used in nightclubs to turn men on, often for money or as a prelude to stripping. Does that mean this particular friend cannot be a feminist? No, because noughtie girl feminism says what is most important is that we are free to make our own choices, which is exactly what she has done. If she felt pressured into pole dancing by men, or because society told her that women have to learn sexy moves, then it might be anti-feminist, but that is not the case.

That doesn't mean that every noughtie girl feminist should pole dance of course, but that if she wants to she can without fearing it will ruin her feminist credentials. She can in fact do whatever it is that she wants, providing it doesn't hurt others, for no other reason than that she wants to – that is the essence of noughties feminism.

The Confession

The thing about feminism is that however much we might aspire to act in a feminist way, most of the time we fall short. I am out and proud as a feminist. But still, I love it when a man buys me dinner. Sometimes when we wake up and my partner suggests that I might like to make him a cup of tea, I not only make it but then I don't throw the scalding liquid over his testicles (after all I am relying on them to give me a baby one day) screaming 'Make your own tea you bastard, I'm a feminist.' Instead I hand it to him with a kiss and a promise that breakfast is coming too.

When, in my single days, I was going to a party and was feeling horny, I would ensure my legs were shaved and my underwear matched. I wanted to be sexy and this meant feminine.

Nor have I always held much regard for the sisterhood. I have been the other woman and got carried away in the heat of the moment, forgetting to feel sorry for the man's partner. If in the future my husband sleeps with another woman I may be hurt, upset and angry but I can't say that I have never been the other woman.

Sometimes when I have wanted something, a refund in a shop perhaps, or a favour from my boss, I have shamelessly and knowingly flirted my way to getting what I wanted. At other times I have deliberately played on the fact that I look young and have a girly voice to get what I want, to seem unthreatening, letting my eyes fill with tears so that people will let me get my own way. Not only that but I like pink and I particularly like glitter.

I have occasionally insisted that a man walks me home to ensure I get back safely, and at other times I have shouted at men for patronising me and suggesting I can't look after myself.

At the DIY shop I say disparaging things about my girly attitude to tools in order for men in the same aisle to come to my aid and help me work out what to buy, and then I take great offence at people who suggest I can't put up a shelf by myself (I can't).

Reader, despite all of this, I am a feminist. It is unrealistic to expect all of us to put being a feminist first all of the time, and even if we did my brand of feminism lets me play on being girly sometimes. Camille Paglia, a famous feminist academic, once gave a lecture at the University of Pennsylvania attended by a friend of mine. She was asked by one of the students whether it was okay to take her husband's surname after marriage to which Paglia replied 'That is just a fishbone in the throat of the feminist revolution.' It's a great line and one that could be applied to any of the day-to-day feminist issues we grapple with.

Take my inability to put up a shelf straight. My lack of DIY skills does not mean I am not a feminist. But I do want the right to put up said shelf should I so wish, buying it with money I have earned myself should I wish to work, and putting it up in a property I own independently should I choose to buy a house. This doesn't mean that I will put up that shelf, or indeed keep my own name, split household tasks with my partner, never look at porn or any of the things that traditional feminists would demand, merely that I demand the right to live with as many choices as men have.

Perhaps the best slogan for feminism, though not necessarily the most eloquent, was the one used by the former Equal Opportunities Commission. It was 'Women. Men. Different. Equal.' This is perhaps more wittily put by the slogan I saw all over South East Asia while backpacking, in which there would be a shop with a similar name to a Western shop, Hanoi Fried Chicken perhaps instead of Kentucky Fried Chicken, and a sign next to it saying 'Same same but different.'

In her book *Full Frontal Feminism*, a rant on why you should be a feminist, Jessica Valenti says:

> *I truly believe that feminism makes your life better. Imagine being able to get past all the nonsense that tells you you're not good enough. To all of a sudden understand why you've ever felt not smart enough or not pretty enough. To finally be able to put your finger on that feeling you've always had that something is off. Believe me, to get to this place is amazing.*

I don't know whether feminism will change your life. Hopefully it is something you can incorporate easily into your existing life. But certainly the intention of feminism is to make lives better, to give everyone an equal shot at achieving anything they want.

Feminism, and noughtie girl feminism in particular, is about acknowledging that we are different while shouting loudly that we are equal. We may not all act in a feminist way all of the time, but if we think we are a feminist, then we are one. Unless of course you are like the woman I know who responded to me asking her whether she was a feminist with a note saying the following: 'I asked my husband whether I am and he said I'm not.' I think it's fair to say that proper feminists do not have to ask their husbands whether they are one.

Further reading

I have found the following books on feminism particularly interesting and helpful in forming my own opinions – you might like them too.

Baumgardner, Jennifer and Richards, Amy, *Manifesta, Young Women, Feminism, and the Future*, Saint Martin's Press Inc, 2001

Kaufman, Gloria (ed.), *In Stitches: Patchwork of Feminist Humour and Satire*, Indiana University Press, 1991

Levy, Ariel, *Female Chauvinist Pigs: Woman and the Rise of Raunch Culture*, Pocket Books, 2006

Mills, Eleanor (ed.) with Cochrane, Kira *Cupcakes and Kalashnikovs: 100 Years of the Best Journalism by Women*, Constable, 2005

Seager, Joni, *The Atlas of Women in the World*, Earthscan Ltd, 2005

Valenti, Jessica, *He's a Stud, She's a Slut and 49 Other Double Standards Every Woman Should Know*, Seal Press, 2008

Valenti, Jessica, *Full Frontal Feminism: A Young Woman's Guide to Why Feminism Matters*, Seal Press, 2007

Walter, Natasha, *The New Feminism*, Virago Press Ltd, 1999

Watkins, Susan et al., *Introducing Feminism*, Icon Books Ltd, 1999

I also suggest the following two websites that have a variety of interesting articles on feminism:

www.thefword.org.uk

www.fawcettsociety.org.uk